Your Ideal Dog

By the same authors

Dog Training: The Gentle Modern Method
Dog Problems: The Gentle Modern Cure

Your Ideal Dog

Teach Your Best Friend to be a Perfect Companion

David Weston and Ruth Weston

Photographs by David Weston

HOWELL
BOOK
HOUSE

New York

Howell Book House
A Simon & Schuster Macmillan Company
1633 Broadway
New York, NY 10019

Library of Congress Cataloging-in-Publication Data

Weston, David, 1929–
     Your ideal dog: teach your best friend to be a perfect companion / David
  Weston and Ruth Weston : photographs by David Weston.
       p. cm.
    ISBN 0–87605–002–X
    1. Dogs—Training. I. Weston, Ruth (Elizabeth Ruth) II. Title.
  SF431.W478   1998   97–46166   CIP
  636.7'0887—dc21

First Howell Book House Edition 1998

10 9 8 7 6 5 4 3 2 1

Photography by David Weston
Photographs on pages 55-7 kindly supplied by Kent and Donna Dannen,
Allenspark, Colorado 80510
Designed and typeset by Rob Cowpe Creative
Printed in China

Many thanks to Dr John Stirling of the Malvern Veterinary Hospital, Isabella the
calf and Mozart the puppy for the photograph on page 15.

Contents

PART 1 People and Dogs

CHAPTER

1	What is an Ideal Dog?	9
2	Educating Your Ideal Dog	12
3	The Right Type of Dog for You	16
4	Being a Responsible Dog Owner in the Twenty-First Century	25
5	Dogs and Children	31
6	Communicating with Your Dog	38
7	The Gentle Modern Method of Dog Training	44
8	How Dogs Learn—The Theory	48
9	Preparing for Training	51

PART 2 The Lessons

How to Train Your Ideal Dog   55

LESSON

1	The Recall	58
2	Sit on Signal	61
3	Stand on Signal	65
4	Drop on Signal	67
5	Stay Still on Signal	69
6	Enjoying Being Touched	74
7	Out for a Walk (Including Doing a Turn)	81
8	Walking Through a Crowd	85
9	Walking Through a Door or Gate	88
10	Remaining Calm when Distractions are Present	90
11	Getting Used to Being Left without the Handler	93
12	Calming Your Dog After Play (Giving up an Article)	96
13	Road Safety (Getting Out of a Car Under Control)	99
14	Meal Time Manners	102

Afterword
Promoting Responsible Dog Ownership 104

Glossary 105

Appendix 106
Assessments
- Ideal Dogs of Australia Assessment (The Kintala Club Inc, Victoria, Australia and The Australian Association of Gentle Modern Dog Training Instructors) 106
- Approved Dog Obedience Assessment Program (Agriculture Victoria; Department of Natural Resources and Environment) 108
- Canine Good Companion Programme (The Canine Association of Western Australia Inc.) 110
- Good Citizen Dog Scheme (The Kennel Club, UK) 111
- Canine Good Citizen Test (The American Kennel Club, USA) 115

PART I
People and Dogs

Chapter 1

What is an Ideal Dog?

What is an 'Ideal Dog'? An 'Ideal Dog' is welcome wherever it goes. It always comes when it is called, walks politely on the lead, sits quietly while it is being groomed or examined by the vet; it doesn't chase cyclists or joggers and is generally a well-behaved member of the community.

An 'Ideal Dog' is a happy dog and this means that you will be happy too. Your neighbours will love a dog that doesn't bark while you are away. Your friends won't get jumped on when they visit you. People and other dogs in the street or park will feel safe when they meet a dog that is under control and has a happy disposition.

Our lifestyle today offers many problems for our dogs which would never have occurred if they had continued to live like their ancestor, the wolf. Wolves have the freedom to travel over vast areas of terrain and they are too busy surviving to have the dubious luxury of becoming bored. In our cities communal living brings about stresses for both man and beast. Our dogs must get used to all kinds of other dogs and people, strange sights and noises. Many of them are left isolated for long periods of the day while the family works, and boredom often leads to the development of behavioural problems such as barking, chewing and digging. What else can we expect?

Just as dogs have to get used to crowds of people, people may have to come into contact with lots of different dogs. Some people would rather not do this because they are frightened of dogs or come from cultures which consider dogs to be dirty. Others may be nervous because they were bitten by a dog as a child.

As dog owners we may feel that we have as much right to take our dogs out to different places as other people have to take their children, but rights carry corresponding responsibilities and we must make sure that our dogs don't upset the non-dog-owners in the community. This is probably not just a responsibility but a necessity; otherwise increasingly harsh dog laws may make it impossible for us to keep a dog in heavily built up areas.

This is where an Ideal Dog programme comes in.

Ideal Dog Programmes

These programmes started in the USA in 1989, partly in response to growing anti-dog feelings among many non-dog-owners. The idea was to give recognition to owners who had a well behaved pet and to show the general public that dogs *can* be 'good citizens'. These

'Canine Good Citizen' programmes, have now been recognised in law by many states in America and have spread overseas to the UK and Australia.

These kinds of courses are available to dogs of all ages, whether they are pure or cross bred. They are great fun for those at both ends of the lead and a terrific way of meeting other responsible dog owners in a non-competitive environment. Most dog owners are not interested in the prolonged formal training which is necessary if they want to compete in obedience trials, yet they want to have a well-mannered pet at home: the Ideal Dog Programme provides the answer.

In Australia, The Kintala Club in Victoria has well-established training courses for both handlers and instructors. We have a firm commitment to teaching the programme using our gentle modern training method, which is explained in the second part of this book. (See also *Dog Training: The Gentle Modern Method* and *Dog Problems: The Gentle Modern Cure*, both written by the authors of this book.) The use of force, such as choker chains, is not allowed. This is particularly important because, if a dog is trained using force, it may end up being either aggressive or fearful. The method also has a flow-through effect on people. It seems that dog owners who use our method become more gentle in their general behaviour, and surely this can only benefit society in general.

Teaching your dog to be an Ideal Dog is relatively easy, particularly if you have some help from a knowledgeable instructor. The courses organised through The Kintala Club have a maximum of six handlers to each instructor so each owner gets a lot of personal attention.

The programme can also help to save the lives of thousands of healthy dogs. We say this because it is an unfortunate fact that the most common cause of premature death in dogs is the development of behaviour problems which often result in a one-way trip to the vet. It would be so much better if people and dogs could learn to live together in harmony.

According to an American humane society, 10.4 million dogs end up in pounds and shelters in the USA every year and 6.3 million are euthanised. These are horrifying statistics, especially when we realise that in all likelihood the majority of these dogs developed behaviour problems due to lack of socialisation and training at the appropriate age and they lost their lives through no fault of their own. We will explain more about socialisation in Chapter 2.

Dogs in the Twenty-first Century

Dogs are becoming increasingly important in our society as companion animals rather than as working stock like sheep or cattle dogs. A study conducted by the Australian Companion Animal Council in 1995 showed that 66 per cent of Australian households have a pet of some kind. Dogs were the most popular, with 68 per cent of owners caring for one or more dog.

Dogs help people in many ways which are often forgotten. When we take our dog for a walk we exercise ourselves as well as the dog and this helps us to avoid all sorts of health problems. Numerous people live by themselves or are alone all day or for weeks at a time when their partner goes away. For them their companion dog may be their only friend and may even help to preserve their sanity. Studies have shown that stroking a dog lowers blood pressure and that dog owners help the economy because they need to visit the doctor less often than people who don't own dogs. It seems a pity that at this time in our history when we are finding new roles for our dogs and learning so much more about them that we should be finding it more and more difficult to keep them in a city or town environment.

Fortunately, most owners are very responsible people and are really keen to do the best they can for their dog. We believe that if they plan well and learn how to train and socialise their dogs then our so-called dog problem could be a thing of the past. Ideal Dog Programmes are an excellent way to teach dog owners how they can live with their dogs in an enjoyable and responsible way.

In order to become an 'Ideal Dog', dogs have to pass an assessment which is slightly different in Australia, the USA and the UK. Details of these tests are given in the Appendix near the end of this book. Most people will find that they can pass the assessment fairly easily once they have completed a recommended course or simply by training their dog using the techniques in this book.

The next three chapters are mostly about puppies,

because there is no doubt that it is much easier to train and socialise a puppy than an adult dog and eventually we hope that all puppies will be brought up to become ideal dogs. However, they do contain information which will be useful to those of you who already have adult dogs and will help with the lessons in the second part of the book. Also we hope that everyone will read Chapters 2 to 4 because we are sure that you or one of your friends will have a new puppy at some stage and forewarned is forearmed!

So what does it take to create the 'Ideal Dog'? It needs education of dog owners, co-operation from local authorities and a modern training system using today's knowledge on animal learning and conditioning which has proved to be highly successful. This is what this book is all about.

Early training and socialisation is the easiest way to create an Ideal Dog

Chapter 2

Educating Your Ideal Dog

Modern canine behaviourists agree with our theory that it is much easier to socialise and train dogs when they are very young rather than attempt to correct problems when they have already developed. It is a bit like the old adage 'give me a child till he's 7 and I'll give you the man.' We could say, 'Give us a dog from 8 to 18 weeks and we'll give you an Ideal Dog!' When we think of how much a human baby learns in its first year we should not be surprised that it is similar for dogs. This is not to say that the child's education should stop at 6 years or the puppy's at 18 weeks, but simply that you will have laid an excellent ground-work for the future.

Because there is an ideal time to teach and socialise dogs you will find it much easier to create your 'Ideal Dog' if you:

1 Get your new dog when it is 7 or 8 weeks old.
2 Start teaching your puppy as soon as it enters your house and try very hard to prevent it from developing any bad habits which will be hard to cure later on.
3 Choose a dog that suits your lifestyle—there are so many breeds and different kinds of dogs available that this is not really a restrictive choice. We discuss the pros and cons of the various breeds in Chapter 3.

If you already have a grown-up dog, don't despair. It can still learn to be your 'Ideal Dog'—you'll just have to spend more time and patience teaching it.

Socialisation

Socialisation is just an easy way of describing how a puppy or child may be helped to adjust to living in our society. It can be defined as 'learning to take part in friendly interchange' or 'making an animal or person suited to fit into society'. Unsocialised dogs are a potential disaster in our densely-populated communities.

We owe most of our knowledge about the socialisation of dogs to Scott and Fuller, two American psychologists who conducted experiments in dog behaviour over a 20-year period during the 1950s and 1960s. The first of their two most important findings was that puppies *must* be socialised, especially during the critical socialisation period which occurs between the third and twelfth week of life. They called it 'critical' because they found that whatever the dogs learnt during that phase of development had a *critical effect on their future behaviour.* They discovered that it is much more difficult to make up for lost time later on in the pup's life.

Puppy School

In 1976 when David founded The Kintala Club he introduced the concept of puppy socialisation and training, starting from 8 weeks of age. We believe that The Kintala Club was the first organisation to do this, although puppy schooling is now offered by a number of organisations and veterinary clinics. For the last 20 years we at The Kintala Club have observed that the puppies rapidly adapt to new experiences up to 12 to 14 weeks of age. If an owner has been advised not to take their pup out from the time of acquisition, usually at 8 weeks of age, until the puppy's immunisation is complete, then it is much harder for the pup to learn to cope with the new things in its life.

What does this mean to the new dog owner? *Firstly it gives you an enormous advantage if you get your puppy at 7 or 8 weeks of age* when the puppy has been weaned and has learnt some social skills within the litter, but at a time when it will quickly adapt to its new environment. Then, as soon as you get the puppy home, you can start introducing it to other pups of a similar size. Ideally this should happen in a structured puppy socialisation class such as the ones we run at The Kintala Club. The Club's contact number is listed in the Appendix. The Club runs a puppy training course where immunised puppies are socialised together before they have their lessons with an accredited instructor. This combination of socialisation and training is ideal for the puppy. It also provides an opportunity for the owners to learn a great deal about their dogs in a friendly, supportive environment. When handlers find that pups can come when

Puppy school

called, sit, stand and lie down on signal, stay in those three positions, heel beside them off lead, and do a basic retrieve after four 20-minute lessons, it is like watching a miracle!

Courses for older dogs

After completing puppy school many people choose to have four more practical lessons in a group and an evening's education session in preparation for an Ideal Dog assessment. At The Kintala Club a certain number of people are then invited to go on to adult socialisation and training classes. The Australian Association of Gentle Modern Dog Training Instructors run 10-week Ideal Dog courses for older dogs which have not been to puppy school.

It is vitally important that you choose a club which teaches using the methods explained in this book and avoid any organisation, or trainer, who says you must use a choker, or correction, chain. The reason for this will be explained in Chapter 8.

Learning about Life

Socialisation with people

As well as meeting other dogs it is important for puppies to meet people of all ages in all sorts of environments—people in wheelchairs, people wearing different types of clothes, people of different cultural backgrounds to your own, all the kinds of people the dog is likely to see in later life. Even the friendliest of dogs is sometimes frightened by people who look different and it will start barking, which is simply the canine way of sounding an alarm. If they meet a cross-section of people as puppies and make friends with them, they are less likely to be a problem when they grow up! The best way to make someone appear friendly and unthreatening to the puppy is to ask them to give it a little piece of food when it greets them. However, you should make absolutely sure that the puppy is behaving appropriately before it is offered food, otherwise you will be rewarding behaviour you don't want.

For instance, most young dogs seem to want to welcome people by jumping up at them and often they find that this is a rewarding experience because they end up by getting patted. In young puppies this may not seem to be much of a problem, but when the puppy grows into an adult it could easily knock

Getting to know people and dogs of different breeds

someone over and cause injury or put dirty paw prints all over their clean clothes! Not the best way to make friends and influence people! Most well-socialised puppies are so exuberantly friendly that they will try to jump up at practically everyone they meet, even strangers. You must never allow a puppy to get into this habit as it can cause a number of problems in later life, even with small dogs.

People are sometimes told to cure this problem by stepping on their dog's rear toes, kneeing the dog in the chest or hitting it across the nose with their hand. Fortunately the most effective remedy is the humane one: anticipate that your dog may jump up and, before it has a chance to do so, call it, induce it to sit, and then reinforce the sit response. Easy! We will show you how to go about it in Lesson 2.

It is particularly important for dogs to get used to children and this also gives adults an opportunity to teach children how to approach and touch dogs. This subject is dealt with in more detail in Chapter 5. Please read this chapter before you introduce your puppy to children!

Socialisation with animals

Learning about other animals is another important part of a puppy's upbringing. Under supervision let it meet cats, chickens, horses, cattle, sheep, or whatever animals it is likely to meet as an adult. Never allow your dog to find out that it is fun to chase them or you will be sorry later!

It is particularly important to make sure that your dog never has the opportunity to chase livestock if you live in the country or the fringes of suburbia. By law all dogs must be confined within their owner's property at all times unless the owner is with them. Some people leave their dogs on an open property under the impression that they stay there all day while the family is at work. These dogs sometimes form a pack with other dogs and then go out hunting and killing. Any dog caught worrying or chasing domestic animals is liable to be shot on sight. It is the owner who deserves to be penalised. Other dogs are left out on the property at night as a guard. Again, how do the owners know if they stay there or not? Please don't fall into this trap.

Needless to say when you are walking your dog it is imperative that you don't allow it to chase native wildlife. If you have trained your dog to come back instantly this is not a problem but, if you can't guarantee this, a long retractable lead will give your dog the freedom to explore under your direct control.

We all need to condition our dogs not to chase (see Lesson 10). The technique is the same whether you are teaching your dog not to chase cyclists, cats or sheep.

Getting your dog used to sights and sounds

We miss out on one of the greatest pleasures in life if we can't take our dogs with us on our outings. The best way to get your dog used to your lifestyle is to take it out with you as much as possible while it is still a puppy. However, your dog will not automatically enjoy travelling with you in the car and you will need to condition it, see Chapter 4.

Puppies must also get used to all the different sounds they are likely to hear during their lives, such as the vacuum-cleaner, lawn-mower, chainsaw, car engine and even people arguing and children screaming. The best way to do this is to introduce the pup to sounds at a distance first of all and then gradually bring them closer while you also increase the volume. If the pup ever looks concerned about noises you can respond by acting confidently yourself and talking to it in a high and happy voice so that you don't make it feel as if there is anything to fear. You may have tried to progress too quickly and you will need to go back to a lower intensity of sound and build up the pup's confidence again. If you marry sounds with pleasure,

Getting to know other animals

Getting to know children

for example dropping a dustbin lid as the puppy eats its food, it will get used to the sounds almost without noticing it! At the same time it will learn that loud noises are beneficial! Lesson 10 will show you how to go about this.

You will find that the socialisation and training of your puppy will be much easier if you choose a breed with a temperament which fits in with your lifestyle. We explore this further in the next chapter.

Chapter 3

The Right Type of Dog for You

The Right Breed

It is generally accepted that wolves have existed for the best part of 3 million years but it was probably not until 10 to 12 thousand years ago that primitive man started domesticating wolf cubs for hunting and defence. A recent study based on genetic material suggests that this date may go back as far as 135,000 years. Since then the interdependence between the two species, man and dog, has developed into the close relationship we have today. People have genetically selected dogs to perform different tasks for them, and have modified their size, coat type and temperament so that the dog is now a very diverse creature.

It stands to reason that when people choose a dog, it should be one which is going to fit into their lifestyle. In simplest terms an elderly person will be happier with a dog that needs less exercise while a regular jogger will want one that needs a great deal!

Herding dogs are great for people who live in the country or who are very active. They are not suited to sedentary flat dwellers, who could well choose a dog like a *Bichon Frise* or *Cavalier King Charles Spaniel*, although these breeds need exercise too.

Terriers have been genetically programmed to be tough, rather feisty, creatures and we don't believe that they are the best choice for people with young children.

Gun dogs are great family dogs and *Golden Retrievers* are ideal pets for most situations. *Labradors* are good fun but they are rather boisterous when young and take a while to mature. *Weimeraners*, *German Shorthaired Pointers* and *Setters* are balls of energy on legs.

German Shepherds are also suitable family dogs, although it is particularly important to socialise them very early and to continue this throughout their lives, otherwise they can become rather tense and nervous. We have also noticed that German Shepherds seem to be orientated towards one particular family member.

The **Spitz breeds** such as the *Samoyed* generally have great temperaments. We have found that *Siberian Huskies* are among the easiest dogs to train while the *Alaskan Malamute* can be a bit sluggish.

Dogs come in many shapes and sizes and their length of coat varies dramatically. We suggest that you don't choose an *Afghan Hound* or *Old English Sheepdog* if you don't have time for grooming!

Some dogs have been specifically bred for fighting. Their strong bodies and exaggerated jaw structure make them formidable opponents when challenged.

Unfortunately they may be triggered into an act of aggression through no fault of their own and the result can be a disaster. We strongly advise you not to choose breeds such as *bull terrier types*, even though we have known many with gentle natures, especially towards people. However, if something goes wrong these dogs can inflict terrible wounds and it's often difficult to get them to release their grip once they have been triggered to bite something, or someone. You may also find that they are greeted with suspicion and feared by many people because of the number of incidents concerning these breeds which have been reported in graphic detail in the media. If you already have a bull terrier type of dog or a cross breed with the same characteristics you will have to be aware of its genetic propensity and train and socialise it very carefully. Another breed that may cause problems is the *Rottweiler*, particularly if it is not socialised appropriately.

Other dogs have different kinds of problems. Breeds with long backs, brachycephalic (short) noses, wrinkled skin, poor teeth and jaw structure or those who can't give birth naturally would never survive in the wild, and in our homes often have short lifespans and attract large veterinary bills. Is it fair to encourage these breeds to be perpetuated?

You will also need to choose a dog which will suit your climate.

A Siberian Husky

A Guide to Choosing your Ideal Dog

The information in the following table may help you to select the breeds that may suit you. Naturally we can't give you very much information in a short book like this, so you will need to do a lot of research yourself. The best place to look at a number of different breeds of dogs is at an all-breeds show or at a training club which accepts all types.

All assessments are based on our experience using the Gentle Modern Method of Training. Dogs trained using compulsion will react unnaturally. The training criteria are based on 3 as the *average* trainability with *our* method. Dogs which score lower than 3 are generally handicapped by physical structure or nervous temperament rather than lacking innate intelligence. Dogs which score higher are generally well structured and have outgoing temperaments.

We have used brackets to indicate that we have some reservations about the suitability of some dogs for families or elderly people. A bracket round (Family) means that the dog is suitable for families with older children who have been educated about how to behave towards dogs. A bracket round (Elderly) means that these dogs are suitable for active older people; they are not suited to a sedentary lifestyle.

These tables can only be a general guide. Dogs are different—just like people—and we have known plenty of dogs which don't conform to the characteristics of their breed!

Small size

Breed	Grooming req.	Temperament	Trainability	Exercise req.	Suitable for
Australian Terrier	Low Strip	Bold	3	Low	Adult Elderly (Family)
Basenji	Low	Flighty	2	Medium	Adult
Bassett Hound	Low	Sound	2	Low	Adult Elderly Family
Beagle	Low	Bold Independent Sound	3	Medium	Adult (Elderly) Family
Bedlington Terrier	Medium Clip	Independent Sound	2	Medium	Adult Elderly Family
Bichon Frise	Medium Clip	Sound	3	Low	Adult Elderly Family
Cocker Spaniel	Medium	Bold Excitable	4	Medium	Adult Elderly
Dachshund	Low	Sound	2	Low	Adult Elderly Family
Maltese Terrier	Medium	Sound	2	Low	Adult Elderly Family
Poodle - Mini	Medium Clip	Excitable Sound	4	Medium	Adult Elderly Family
Poodle - Toy	Medium Clip	Excitable Sound	3	Low	Adult Elderly Family
Pug	Low	Bold Sound	2	Low	Adult Elderly Family

cont'd

Breed	Grooming req.	Temperament	Trainability	Exercise req.	Suitable for
Schnauzer - Mini	Medium Strip	Bold	3 to 4	Medium	Adult Elderly (Family)
Scottie	Medium Clip	Bold	2 to 3	Low	Adult Elderly
Shih Tzu	High	Sound	2	Low	Adult Elderly Family
Skipperke	Low	Sound	3	Medium	Adult Elderly Family
West Highland White Terrier	Medium Strip	Bold	3	Medium	Adult Elderly
Whippet	Low	Reserved	2	Med/High	Adult (Family)

Medium size

Breed	Grooming req.	Temperament	Trainability	Exercise req.	Suitable for
Border Collie	Med/High	Active Excitable	5	High	Adult (Family)
Boxer	Low	Active Excitable	3	High	Adult (Family)
Briard	Medium	Active Excitable	3	Medium	Adult Family
Brittany Spaniel	Medium	Active Sound	3	Medium	Adult Elderly Family
Bull Terrier	Low	Bold	2	Medium	Not Recom- mended

cont'd

Breed	Grooming req.	Temperament	Trainability	Exercise req.	Suitable for
Cattle Dog	Low	Active Excitable	4	High	Adult
Collie	High	Reserved	3	High	Adult Family
Curly Coated Retriever	Medium	Sound	3	Medium	Adult Elderly Family
Dalmatian	Low	Active Excitable Sound	4	High	Adult Family
German Shorthaired Pointer	Low	Active Excitable	5	High	Adult Family
Golden Retriever	Medium	Sound	5	Medium	Adult Elderly Family
Keeshond	High	Sound	3	Medium	Adult Elderly Family
Kelpie	Low	Active Excitable	5	High	Adult Family
Labrador	Low	Sound	5	Medium	Adult Elderly Family
Samoyed	Medium	Independent Sound	3	Medium	Adult Family
Schnauzer-Standard	Medium Strip	Bold	3	Medium	Adult Family
Shetland Sheepdog	High	Excitable Reserved	4	Medium	Adult Elderly Family
Siberian Husky	Medium	Independent Sound	5	High	Adult Family

cont'd

Medium size cont'd

Breed	Grooming req.	Temperament	Trainability	Exercise req.	Suitable for
Springer Spaniel	Medium	Active Sound	4	Medium	Adult Elderly Family
Staffordshire Bull Terrier	Low	Bold	2	Medium	Not Recommended

Large size

Breed	Grooming req.	Temperament	Trainability	Exercise req.	Suitable for
Afghan Hound	High	Flighty Reserved	1	Medium	Adult Family
Alaskan Malamute	Medium	Bold	2	Medium	Adult (Family)
Bernese Mountain Dog	Medium	Reserved	2 to 3	Low/Med	Adult Family
Bull Mastiff	Low	Sound	2	Low/Med	Adult (Family)
Doberman Pinscher	Low	Flighty	3 to 4	High	Adult (Family)
German Shepherd	Medium	Reserved	4 to 5	Med/High	Adult (Family)
Great Dane	Low	Sound	1 to 2	Medium	Adult (Family)
Irish Setter	Medium	Flighty	2 to 3	Med/High	Adult Family
Mastiff	Low	Sound	1	Low/Med	Adult Family

cont'd

Breed	Grooming req.	Temperament	Trainability	Exercise req.	Suitable for
Newfoundland	Med/High	Sound	4	Medium	Adult Family
Old English Sheepdog	High	Excitable	2	Medium	Adult (Family)
Poodle - Standard	Medium Clip	Excitable	3 to 4	High	Adult (Family)
Rottweiler	Low	Bold	5	Medium	Adult (Family)
Schnauzer - Giant	Medium Strip	Bold	3 to 4	Medium	Adult (Family)

Cross-Bred or Pure-Bred?

It is easier to predict the future temperament of a puppy if you buy a pure-bred dog. A cross between two breeds of known temperament can also work out very well. This is not to say that mongrel dogs are necessarily temperamentally unsound. Clearly that would be a ridiculous statement. However, we have met so many people who did not realise the genetic potential of their dog and ended up with a big problem on their hands, that we cannot recommend that you take that risk.

For the same reasons you should be extremely careful if you want to choose a puppy from an animal shelter. Don't let your heart rule your head and remember the puppy will be part of your life for years. It is usually safer to buy a puppy from a reliable breeder.

Breeders

Breeders sometimes select the parents of their puppies for looks rather than temperament or working ability because they want to be successful at shows. Try to choose a breeder who produces balanced dogs. Looks are not very important as long as the dog is structurally sound.

It is very important to research the common inherited problems in the various breeds. The parents of the puppy you choose should have been adequately screened, for example the hips should have been X-rayed in breeds which commonly develop hip dysplasia. Responsible breeders will be happy to talk to you about this. However, a word of warning: some breeders may accentuate virtues and minimise problems so try to get a cross-section of opinions.

Choose a breeder who will answer your questions and expect to be interrogated in return. Breeders want to make sure that *you* are a suitable owner. A problem may arise if a breeder wants to keep a few of the 'better' pups in the litter until well past the age when it is best for the puppy to go to its new home (see Chapter 2). We believe that nothing is more important than getting the puppy at 7 or 8 weeks of age and if the breeder will not release the pup you want, then you should look elsewhere.

Sometimes a breeder will offer you a puppy free of charge in return for the right to breed from it at a later date. This can have far-reaching ramifications and is probably not a good idea for the novice dog owner.

Pet Shops

Most pet shops concentrate on the sale of pet products. However, some do sell livestock and the bright-eyed puppy in the window can be a great attraction. Unfortunately, pet shop proprieters are unlikely to know the background and circumstances of the animals that come to them for sale and it is doubtful that the pups would have been sold to these outlets if the litter had been planned and cared for in the first place. We have seen a great deal of heartache caused by buying a puppy which becomes sick, or dies, soon after the new owner takes it home.

Male or Female?

Choosing a puppy from a large group can be hard. It will be easier if you make the decision about whether you want a male or female dog before you go to see a litter, so that you only need to select from one sex.

Males tend to be more energetic, have a strong sex drive after puberty, may be inclined to wander and are often more aggressive with other males. Intact male dogs are often a problem in densely populated areas. Their levels of the male hormone, testosterone, urge them to 'Go out and look for a mate and challenge any other intact male dog who gets there before you'. In a social hierarchy like a wolf pack, aggression is controlled by an elaborate display of body language between the members of each sex. There are separate male and female hierarchies and each member of the pack knows its own place in the group structures and does not normally challenge a higher placed wolf. Dogs rarely have the opportunity to live in a pack and even if groups of domestic dogs meet regularly it is a fallacy to suggest that they form a wolf-like group. A hierarchy is only formed within a stable population who live together continuously.

Male dogs in our society have an added problem. They are fertile all year round whereas male wolves are only fertile for about four months out of twelve. Female wolves come into season once a year at approximately the same time as each other. Female dogs often have two seasons per year and this can occur at different times so potentially there may be females who are ready to mate throughout the year! This makes it difficult for the poor male dogs! If you don't intend to breed from a male dog, it is better to have him castrated prior to puberty so that he never gets into the pattern of adult male sexual behaviour. Desexed males are much easier to manage and cannot contribute to the thousands of unwanted dogs which are born each year.

Females will usually wander only when they are in season, are less energetic and often have a gentler disposition. However, we have been told of two female wolves having a prolonged and bloody fight when they both had litters of puppies. If you are going to have more than one dog, it is probably better to choose one of either sex. However, if your animals are spayed or castrated this is of less importance.

Choosing a Puppy

Before you get to this stage you should have made sure that you have the time, commitment, energy and finances to cope with a dog. Can you make arrangements for someone to look after the dog if you are sick or on holiday? Chapters 2 and 4 will give you some idea of the kind of contingencies you will have to cover.

Assuming that you still want a puppy, you can find out where litters are available from your local breeders' association. Home breeders will often advertise in local papers. Try to make your enquiries at an early stage before too many puppies have been selected so that you can get the one you want. Good breeders often have waiting lists for pups. Presuming you have already decided whether you want a male or a female pup, you can then gauge their temperament. The likelihood is that the pups will be like their parents, especially the mother who does most of the rearing, so try to meet the parents, too. Avoid getting a puppy if either parent shows signs of nervousness or aggression, as the pups may well inherit these traits.

Watch the pups playing for a while and do not select any pup that always appears to be on top of the others or any that show timidity. Even at an early age you can usually tell who is at the top and

the bottom of the hierarchy. Choose one from the middle of the range.

Call the pups to you. The puppy you want should be very attracted to people. You can also try picking each puppy up. Avoid any that struggle madly or bite at your hands. If you are keen to have a dog that retrieves, you can toss a soft sock for them one at a time and see which ones have a natural tendency to chase and pick up an article. You will not be able to assess this accurately until the puppies are at least 7 to 8 weeks old because their eyesight will not be fully developed until then.

Which puppy?

If none of the pups appears right for you, don't be afraid to say so. The pup is hopefully going to share your life for many years and you want it to be just right.

In the next chapter we will discuss how to organise the early days of your relationship with your new friend.

Being a Responsible Dog Owner in the Twenty-First Century

Preparing for your Puppy

Having chosen the breed you want and the particular pup you like, it's now time to plan ahead for its homecoming.

1 Is your garden secure? You can't raise a puppy successfully if you're not able to confine it safely. If you have a very large property, you can fence off a section, but it should be big enough to give the puppy freedom to explore.

Even if you live on a very big property in the country you must have a secure place where you can leave your dog so that it will not get into mischief when you are away. Traditionally country dogs are left chained up, but this may make them aggressive, so it is better to give them a run with a kennel.

2 Get grooming tools, dishes for water and food, and a collar with an identity tag and a long, light lead before you pick your puppy up. Ideally you will not be using the lead for the first two or three weeks until you have taught your puppy to walk nicely beside you off the lead (see Lesson 7).

3 Try to arrange to have some time at home with your new puppy. If you are working, take a holiday. Puppies don't like being left alone and you will want to spend as much time as you can

taking your puppy out and about and socialising it (see Chapter 2). This is the best time for establishing a life-long friendship with your new companion.

The First Day

Try to collect your puppy early in the day so that it has time to get used to its new home before dark. If possible, avoid long-distance travel but, if you do have to cover a fair distance, break your journey approximately every hour so that the puppy can eliminate and get a bit of fresh air and exercise. Sometimes air travel is less traumatic for a puppy than a long car ride.

When you arrive home, it is very important that your new pup is introduced to any other dog in the household on neutral ground, for instance in a nearby park. Perhaps a friend or family member could help. Allow the dogs to meet and then they can go home together. An established dog will accept the newcomer much more readily if you do this than if you simply bring the new pup into its 'territory' straight away. Watch them at first but don't interfere unless the older dog seems intolerant and is likely to injure

Using the doggy door

Introducing your puppy to your adult dog

the puppy. Most puppies will pester older dogs and the older dog must be allowed to tell the puppy when it is tired of play. It will do this with a growl or perhaps a snap, just like the pup's mother did, and the pup will soon learn. Don't panic if it squeals and lies on its back as this is natural, too.

Let the pup have a good explore of the house under supervision, then it will probably be due for a meal and a long sleep!

Getting to Know One Another

Don't fall into the trap of isolating your puppy in one room or putting it outside for long periods on its own. Dogs are social creatures and they need company. Your puppy can learn to stay in a playpen or a small enclosure on its own for short periods of time and, of course, it has to get used to the idea that you will not be there constantly. But if you expose a young puppy to long periods of isolation it will become stressed and this will lead to the development of behavioural problems such as digging, pulling washing off the line, whimpering or barking. Like children, *dogs need to feel secure before they can spend too much time alone.*

Later on, if you have to be away a lot, you may like to consider getting another dog or a cat to keep your dog company.

Barking

Dogs who bark incessantly usually do so because they are bored or stressed. The best solution is to have a doggy door installed. This is a small opening through a wall or window where a dog can enter but which is too small for a burglar! Doggy doors have the great benefit that your dog can choose to be either inside or outside when you are not at home. The dog does not necessarily have to have the run of the house—entry to a kitchen or laundry is fine. Your dog is less likely to be bored if it can have a change of scenery. Also, if you leave a radio on, it will help to mask some of the neighbourhood noises which could stir up your dog and make it bark.

Barking dogs is one of the most frequently encountered 'behaviour' problems and one which is easily solved with a bit of commonsense. For more information about this topic, we refer you to our book *Dog Problems: The Gentle Modern Cure.*

It is best to install the doggy door and teach your pup to use it during those first few weeks when you

Meeting the postwoman

are at home. Then, gradually over a number of days get it used to being left alone. Of course, when you are home your dog will be much happier if it is inside with you.

First Lessons

We suggest that you start house-training your puppy, get it used to its name, and teach it to come when it is called right from the first day, see Lesson 1.

Introductions

It is an excellent idea to introduce your new arrival to your neighbours, the postman and anyone else who regularly calls at your house. Most people can't resist a puppy and even those who are not too keen on dogs will find a little puppy is not much of a threat. They can then build up a relationship as the dog matures and will be more likely to help you rather than complain if your dog barks too much one day, for example.

Food

If you want to change the puppy's diet, do this over a period of a few days so that it gets used to it gradually. An 8-week-old puppy needs a maximum of three meals a day and this should be cut down to two as soon as it loses interest in one of the meals, or by 10 to 12 weeks of age at the latest.

Sometimes people are advised to feed their pup

much too frequently and many dogs become obese as a result. Pups which put on too much weight too early are also prone to joint problems such as elbow or hip dysplasia. We recommend that you get down to one meal a day from about 3 to 4 months of age. Consult your veterinarian if you are worried about your puppy's weight. We are aware that this is an area of concern for many new dog owners so we have included more information about the importance of a good feeding regime in Chapter 9.

Grooming

Grooming your dog should be a pleasurable experience for you both. It is important to start brushing and handling your puppy right from the first day. We show you how you can condition your dog to enjoy it in Lesson 6. You may also have to trim your dog's nails unless it runs on hard surfaces regularly. If you don't know how to do this get an expert to show you or you might hurt your dog and make it nervous about having its feet touched in the future. During grooming you should check your dog for burrs, grass seeds and any lumps and bumps in, or under, the skin. Also check the mammary glands of both males and females and the testicles of males if they are still present. Most vets recommend that male dogs are castrated by 6 months of age.

A Visit to the Vet

During the first few days take your new puppy to your veterinarian. Check on its immunisation and find out if you are doing the right thing with your worming and flea control. You will have to take your dog to the vet at least once a year for booster immunisation and in some places you may have to give it heartworm tablets. Make sure that you know exactly what you must do to keep your dog healthy by asking your vet what is needed in your particular geographical area.

It is a great idea to have your veterinarian's emergency number in a readily accessible place in the house and find out how to get help outside normal business hours, as this could save your dog's life one day. In case of emergency, it is usually better to phone the vet and let the clinic know that you are on your

way and what the problem is. They can then be prepared for your arrival.

Animal treatment can be very costly, as most people do not have health insurance for their dogs in the same way they may for themselves. We suggest that you consider saving a bit of money every week for emergency veterinary care, especially if funds are tight. Local humane societies or veterinary colleges usually provide treatment more cheaply.

Exercise

Regular exercise is necessary for all animals if they are to remain physically and psychologically healthy. It is also part of your puppy's socialisation programme and you should start taking it for walks right from the first day you have it at home. Dogs need daily opportunities to meet other dogs, smell doggy odours and generally run and play off lead, but this obviously brings about attendant responsibilities. For instance, you cannot let your dog off the lead if it will not come back when it is called! Before 12 weeks of age, it is natural for wolves and dogs to stay close to their family group because they are not big enough and bold enough to do anything else! If you have a young dog you can capitalise on the period between 8 and 12 weeks and condition it to come when called (see Lesson 1).

Older dogs who are in the habit of running off will

Examination at the vet's

need to be retrained in a restricted environment first of all.

In all probability your dog will want to urinate and defecate when it is out for a walk but there is nothing which can raise the ire of both dog owners and non-dog owners alike than seeing a large pile of faeces deposited on their front lawn or stepping in 'poo' on the footpath!

Please carry something to pick up your dog's faeces and encourage your local authority to provide doggy poo bins.

Then everyone will be happy.

Local Dog Laws

It is true to say that just one person who breaks a law can spoil the freedom of many. We should all consider ourselves ambassadors for dogs when we take our pets out. Their behaviour should encourage non-doggy people to think that dogs and dog owners really are all right! So if a notice says 'Dogs on Lead' either obey the sign, or go elsewhere where you can let your dog go free without offending anybody.

It is sensible to put your dog on the lead near play equipment and sporting grounds whether this is required by law or not. In Australia dogs still have a relative amount of freedom but this will quickly disappear as it has done in the USA and UK if dog owners are not seen to act responsibly.

The requirements for registering your dog vary in different countries, municipalities and states. Your local governing body will be happy to provide you with details if you contact them.

Identify your Dog

There is a big movement towards establishing an international standard for the identification of animals through microchips which are inserted under the skin. The advantage of a microchip is that it is a permanent form of identification which cannot be removed, stolen or lost. Your local veterinarian or animal shelter can advise you where you can get this done.

However, even if your dog has been microchipped, it should wear a fixed collar with an identity tag at all times. A tag can be read by anyone without the

benefit of a scanner and, of course, a lead can be clipped to the collar. With all the care in the world, dogs occasionally get out of their homes, for example, the meter man may leave the gate open.

Travelling

Some dogs, particularly puppies, become carsick. At first, this is probably due to the irregular motion of the vehicle, but the fear and anxiety associated with feeling nauseated may become a habit if left untreated.

Here's how you can help:
1 Try feeding your puppy every meal in the car while it is stationary so that it associates the car with the pleasure of eating. If it is big enough, try to get it to jump into the car rather than picking it up and placing it there. Then it will be rewarded by its own voluntary action.
2 When you have done this for a few days, try driving a *short distance* to a local park where you can take your puppy for a walk, so that once again the car is associated with fun. You can gradually build up the distance you cover.
3 You could consider giving your dog a mild sedative if you cannot avoid driving long distances when it is very young. Ask your veterinarian about this.

Driving with unrestrained dogs can be dangerous.

A divider makes travelling much safer

Holidays

It is a good idea to install a seat belt for your dog or place a divider between the seats and the back of the car. Under no circumstances should your dog be loose in the front seat beside the driver where it could interfere with driving or affect the controls.

Holidays

If it is possible, we suggest that you take your dog on holiday with you. However, there are times when this is impractical. Probably the best solution is to have a friend come and stay at your home and care for your animals for you. If this is impossible you will need to look for a reputable kennel and book well in advance. Your dog will be happier if you choose a kennel which provides some exercise and where your dog can play

with other socialised dogs for part of the day. Obviously the kennel should be clean, and the owners genuinely fond of the animals in their care. Kennels will quite rightly insist that your dog's vaccinations are up to date.

We do not recommend that you leave your dog at home alone with a neighbour to feed it unless it is just for one night. Dogs are social animals and they need company. Never leave a puppy alone even for one night.

Train your Dog to be an Ideal Dog See Part Two.

There is certainly a lot to think about if we want to have an ideal dog, but with a little time and effort, especially when our dogs are young, we will be rewarded with friendship for a lifetime. In Chapter 6 we discuss how to communicate with our canine friends. The next chapter is all about dogs and children.

Chapter 5

Dogs and Children

Why do we need a special chapter on children and dogs? The answer is that our Ideal Dog should behave well with everyone and in every situation, not only with adults. However, although the relationship between a child and a dog can be the best thing in both their lives, it can also go tragically wrong.

This chapter is meant for everyone—whether they have a child, a dog, or both. People who are in charge of children should know how to teach them to avoid trouble with dogs. Conversely, dog owners who don't have children have a responsibility to teach their dogs to be safe around children. The next few pages will explain how to go about this.

A child and a dog can be an ideal combination. Dogs are non judgemental and keep secrets well! They always welcome you and never get angry when you misbehave. Many of us can remember the fun we had with our dogs when we were children. How we played with them and loved them and how they comforted us when we were in trouble. However, we probably don't remember the care our parents took to teach us and our dogs how to behave towards each other.

Remember our three suggestions for creating the Ideal Dog? If your dog is going to live with children you will need to be even more careful to carry them out and even add a few more.

1 It is even more important that your dog is well socialised with other dogs and gets used to children as well as adults from 8 weeks of age.

Please don't be tempted to offer a home to an older dog unless you know its previous history and that it has lived with children in the past and got on well with them.

2 Your choice of dog is more important than ever. Preferably select a passive type of family dog such as a Golden Retriever, Newfoundland, Shih Tzu or Cavalier King Charles Spaniel. Never choose as a family dog one which has been bred for attack work such as a Bull terrier, Staffordshire bull terrier or pit bull terrier type.

3 You should avoid leaving babies or pre school children alone with a dog *at any time*.

4 Supervise children when they are with dogs up until the age of 10 or 11.

The Children in the Pack

Why do we need to take these extra precautions with children and dogs? Remember that, although our dogs live with humans, to a certain extent they still think like wolves not people. In a pack a wolf learns to accept its position through a natural process of learning. Puppies are not able to challenge bigger adult wolves so they learn that being submissive will avert any potential aggression towards them. They also learn that if they challenge other puppies in play some may be submissive and some superior to them. And so they find their own position in the hierarchy.

In our homes our dogs will try to find their place in our family hierarchy in just the same way. Most dogs will readily accept their subordinate position if they have been sensibly trained by their human pack. We don't have to use force to establish our superiority, just be consistent and follow the suggestions outlined in the earlier chapters of this book. When we train a dog to respond to our signals we naturally assume a high status in the dog's eyes.

However, children, especially babies and toddlers, are not physically capable of behaving like an adult person so the dog may regard them as inferior. They may even try to discipline them in a dog-like way, usually with a growl and occasionally with a quick nip. If the child accepts the dog's warning and stops teasing it, no great harm will be done, but if the child becomes frightened, screams and tries to run away the dog's hunting instincts may be triggered off and it may start to chase the child and even bite.

Luckily this very rarely happens, which says much for the goodwill which exists between children and dogs. However, adults should be aware that it *may* happen, and this is why young children and dogs should never be left alone together.

Misunderstandings are more likely to happen with babies and toddlers who are too young to be taught sensible behaviour towards dogs. This is why many people advise parents not to get a dog until their youngest child is at least 6 years old. If the parents already have an older dog they will need to condition it to accept the baby as suggested later in the chapter.

Educating Children and Dogs

What can we do to ensure that all children are safe when they come into contact with dogs? After all we have to look at things in perspective. We cannot be so concerned about the problems that we miss out on all the benefits that dogs have to offer.

At The Kintala Club, where gentleness is the rule, dogs are raised from puppyhood to interact with each other and with members and their families. Parents bring their children in prams, back packs and on foot, and older children help with the training. There is constant supervised interaction between parents, children and dogs.

We believe that children should be taught about animal care at home and at school, just as they are taught about road safety. Once there was no need to teach road safety because cars were few and far between, once most children learnt about dogs as a matter of course because dogs lived in relative freedom and children met them in most suburban streets. Because dogs now have to be kept behind fences they are often not familiar with children and they have to be taught how to relate to them, while children in turn have to be taught how to behave towards dogs. This is the importance of socialisation. If we do not consciously educate both children and dogs, the misunderstandings between them will continue and both children and dogs will suffer.

Some authorities are trying to deal with the problem of dog attacks by labelling some breeds of dog as dangerous but this does little to solve the problem. However, as we have stated earlier, we strongly believe that anyone with children should not consider acquiring one of the breeds which have been bred to attack. Rules that keep dogs under constant restraint will not work either. Dogs that don't get plenty of exercise feel bored and bad-tempered and are much more likely to cause an incident than happy healthy dogs. Most dogs who have injured children have done so because they were not raised and trained appropriately or the children concerned did not know how to behave towards dogs.

All dogs in our society should be trained and socialised at a very young age under the supervision of

Don't approach a dog from behind!

This is the right way to approach a strange dog.

A study conducted in Australia between 1988 and 1994 by Monash University's Accident Research Centre showed that 80 per cent of children who were bitten by dogs were bitten in their own home or the home of a friend, and that children under 5 constituted 43 per cent of all dog attacks. In total 1916 people attended hospital after receiving dog bites during the 6-year study period. These statistics are a terrible indictment of both parents and dog owners. We should cooperate in the education of children and dogs instead of blaming each other for the accidents. Every time we meet each other outside our homes it is an opportunity to teach 'dog safety'. The following hints will help.

Teaching Children about Dogs

1 Teach young children that puppies and dogs need a place of their own to sleep undisturbed during parts of the day. It is tempting for a youngster to pounce on a sleeping dog, which is likely to jump out of the way but could possibly snap; either way the child may get hurt. This is more likely to happen with a dog that has poor hearing.

Let sleeping dogs lie (especially if they are old and rather deaf)!

experienced instructors. It is terribly important that they are trained in a humane manner as explained in this book so that the method of training itself does not provoke aggression. Unfortunately we still see children jerking their dogs with choker chains and shouting at them. No wonder we end up with dogs who are suspicious about people and who are likely to attack if provoked or frightened.

2 If you have a puppy, show children how to sit on the floor and hold it in their laps. They should be taught to remain reasonably passive so that it doesn't get excited.

3 Remember that pre school children may think of dogs as fluffy toys and not understand the possible consequences of teasing or hurting them. It is just as important to teach them that dogs are living

Supervised quiet play allows children and dogs to get to know each other.

Ballgirl!

creatures who feel pain in the same way as we do as it is to teach them to avoid fire.

4 Make sure that small children remain reasonably quiet when they are playing with a dog or puppy. They often throw their arms up in the air in excitement when they are playing. This can stimulate a dog to jump up and investigate, and the child could get knocked over or inadvertently scratched or nipped. It is even worse if children scream and run because they are then acting like a prey animal from the dog's point of view. This can lead to disastrous consequences.

5 Show children how to approach dogs from a front/side angle and never from the rear.

6 Encourage small children to take a turn at training the family dog. By calling the dog and giving it a piece of food, the child becomes friends with it and will have some control over its behaviour.

7 Take children and dogs on walks and family outings together.

8 Teach your dog to fetch, bring back and give up an article (see Lesson 12). Children and dogs can then play any number of ball games. Dogs make excellent ball boys, fielders, wicket keepers, goalies, etc. *and never want a turn with the bat!* Remember to make sure that children use a soft ball when they play with dogs.

9 Under no circumstances should you allow children to poke at, play tug of war with or tease a dog in any way, including pulling its tail.

10 Tell children *never* to pat a dog which is frightened, angry, injured, tied up, sleeping, eating or playing with a toy. Even the gentlest dog may react instinctively and BITE! This does not mean that you can't teach your own dog to happily accept a child approaching the food bowl or taking a toy from it. However, not all dog owners teach their dogs to accept this so it is safer to teach children to behave safely with *all* dogs.

11 Don't let a small child take a dog for a walk on its own. Teenagers will enjoy the responsibility of exercising their dog in a safe area **away from traffic**.

12 Don't force your dog to make friends with children if it doesn't want to. Some dogs are frightened of children because they find them noisy and unpredictable. They will normally avoid children and they should be allowed to do this. Admit honestly that your dog doesn't like children and keep it away from them.

A *frightened* dog looks like this — don't touch it.

A dog which is tied up may feel threatened and bite.

Let your dog eat in peace.

Don't try to take prized possessions away from strange dogs.

Teenagers enjoy taking their dog for a run.

Meeting Strange Dogs

So far we have been talking about family dogs in the home where an adult can supervise both dogs and children. However, how should children react to the strange dogs they may meet in the park or street? All dogs who are outside their own homes should be accompanied by a responsible person—this is the law in most places, but unfortunately a few people think that laws are made to be broken!

1 Children should be taught that every dog they meet will not want to be friends with them. It is best to teach them to ask the handler of a dog whether they may pat it.

2 If the handler tells them not to go near the dog or the dog runs away *they should leave it alone.*

3 Tell children that dogs may bite even when they are on the lead. In fact this is more likely to happen because the lead stops the dog from pulling away and it may feel 'cornered'.

4 Never allow children to tease dogs which are confined in people's gardens, e.g. by poking sticks at them or making a noise. The dog may meet the child in the road another day and remember who teased it, or it may begin to dislike children in general.

5 Teach children not to try to separate fighting dogs. They should find an adult to help.

6 If a child is approached by a strange dog it may be because the child is carrying something that the dog wants. If the child puts the item down on the ground where the dog can see it and then walks slowly away, the dog will probably go to it and lose interest in the child. Or the dog may be curious because the child is running around and making a lot of noise. If so, the child should become *quiet* and *still* and keep its hands at its sides. When the dog loses interest, the child should move away slowly and report the incident to an adult.

7 If a dog jumps up and knocks a child over, the child should curl up in a ball, put its hands behind its neck and remain *quiet* until the dog moves away. Of course, this isn't necessary if the child knows the dog is friendly and it has simply pushed the child over accidentally during play.

This dog is aggressive.
Don't go near it!

The Aggressive Dog

Adults often ask how they should react when faced with an aggressive dog. Let's face it, it can happen, so we should teach children what to do if it occurs.

We recommend that you teach children that dogs will make themselves look bigger when they want to look aggressive. They raise their heads and tails, their hair stands on end and they will try to stare their 'opponent' down. The dog may growl and show its teeth and sound very menacing. A dog which is ready to attack will lower its body and head in preparation for springing. Children should avoid these dogs if possible but, if a child *is* approached by an aggressive dog, the secret is to teach them to look the opposite of the aggressive dog. They should make themselves as small and quiet as possible, and avoid eye contact with the dog but still watch what it is doing. The shoulders should drop low and the hands should be kept quiet and still at the child's side. The child should be instructed to back away very slowly or move sideways if it thinks it can get into a safe place away from the dog's reach. *The child should not run away.*

If the dog attacks, the child should be told to drop to the ground in a foetal position and place its hands over the back of its neck as in item 7. From a dog's point of view this is pure submission and it should end the attack. It also protects the vital organs. The child should stay in this position until the dog loses interest and moves away.

It is most unlikely that even the most aggressive

dog will attack a person (child or adult) unless it is provoked, i.e. it feels its territory is being invaded, it is being teased or it is overexcited. Children should be taught to leave strange dogs alone and they will have no reason to be frightened.

Introducing your Dog to a New Baby

Although we have suggested that people with a young family do not acquire a dog until their youngest child is about 6 years old, there are many families who manage to cope with any number of young children and dogs who all play happily together. Then there are other people who already share their lives with dogs and want to start a family. This is not usually too much of a problem if the dog is treated sensibly and prepared for the baby's arrival.

Some parents think that it is better to keep their dog in the garden once a new baby has arrived. We feel that this is likely to cause a great many problems, as dogs which are not allowed to be part of the family are highly likely to develop all sorts of behaviour problems. However, if you have made this decision you should plan well ahead. Any changes in the dog's routine should be well established before the new baby comes home so that the dog does not associate the baby with these changes. Even dogs don't react well to having their privileges withdrawn!

We suggest that you introduce your baby to your dog in the following way:

1 If the baby is born in a hospital, it is helpful if someone takes home an item of clothing which the baby has worn so that the dog can become accustomed to the baby's smell.
2 When the new baby arrives home it may be carried in its mother's arms or perhaps lie in a carry cot. Another member of the family should sit the dog beside Mum or the carry cot and give it some food.

The sight and smell of the baby will then be associated in the dog's mind with great benefit. This will only take a few minutes but is well worth the effort although it may be the last thing the new parents want to do at that particular time!

3 Next allow the dog to watch the baby and sniff it gently. *Monitor them at all times.*
4 For the first few days the baby should be in the room when the dog gets fed and you should only pat the dog when the baby is present so that all good things happen in the presence of the baby.
5 When you want to put your dog outside, do so *before* you pick the baby up.
6 Never punish your dog for picking up the baby's toys. The smell of the baby must not be associated with anything which is unrewarding. Simply take the toy away and wash it thoroughly and give the dog one of its *own* toys. Prevention is the best strategy!
7 When the baby starts to crawl, you must watch it all the time. Babies can pull the dog's hair and poke their little fingers where they are not supposed to go and it is *natural* for a dog to react by growling a warning. Unfortunately the baby will not understand. It is actually amazing that dogs are so tolerant.
8 As soon as the child is old enough, you should teach it to handle the dog correctly. A 4 year old should be able to teach a dog to come when called and reward it.

It is really a matter of common sense. The vast majority of dogs are wonderful companions. The few who are not have not had the benefit of a good education. If you train your dog to be an 'Ideal Dog' it will be your friend for life and just as importantly everyone else will think it is a great dog too.

Remember that dog attacks are nearly always the result of lack of appropriate education and supervision.

Communicating with Your Dog

Most of us can communicate with each other fairly effectively, but we may not know much about relating to animals. It stands to reason that, if we want to influence a dog's behaviour, we should learn how to communicate with it in the most effective way. For example, you are reading this book at the moment to learn how you can teach your dog to be well behaved, but if you put the book in front of your dog it wouldn't learn much. We use language as a major means of communication with other people and rely less on body language and gesture, although these certainly play a part. Dogs, on the other hand, rely *mostly* on body language and gesture.

Whether we are human or dog, we use our senses of sight, hearing, smell, touch and taste to learn about the world around us.

Dogs have inherited senses which have been perfected for survival by their ancestor, the wolf. Let's look at these senses one at a time.

The Sense of Sight

Contrary to popular opinion, the most important sense in a wild or domesticated dog is sight. Every moment it is awake, the dog is aware of its surroundings. Dogs are often called 'colour blind', but that

term has proven to be very misleading. A PhD study in the USA has shown that dogs can see the same range of colours as a person who suffers from a condition called deuteranopia, that is, red/green blindness. Dogs can see colours at one end of the spectrum very well, that is blue, indigo and violet. Bluey-green appears to them as white, while all other colours are seen as shades of yellow.

We can conclude that the ability to see a large range of colours is relatively unimportant to wolves and dogs. On the other hand, it is terribly important for wolves to see in a dim light so that they can hunt effectively at twilight. Superior night sight has been developed at the expense of colour vision and this ability has been passed on to our domestic dogs. We on the other hand, as hunter gatherers in the past, needed excellent colour vision so that we could find brightly coloured berries and fruits to eat and distinguish whether they were edible or poisonous.

Vision does not rely on colour alone and dogs compensate for their inferior colour vision with a remarkable ability to see the slightest movement. Their eyes are set slightly to the side of their heads which allows them to have a much wider view than we do, because our eyes are set at the front of our head. Their cornea and lens are much larger than ours which also helps.

Above, a human's eyes and
below, a dog's eyes

On the other hand their long noses prevent them from seeing well with both eyes simultaneously and, as a result, their ability to focus at a short distance is poor. If a dog sees you throw a piece of food 3 or 4 metres (9 or 12 feet) away, it will immediately race to the approximate place where the food landed, then proceed to sniff all around the area until it finds the food by using its sense of smell. In contrast, most humans have excellent binocular vision and as a result we can see to design and manipulate the most intricate pieces of machinery, read books, perform surgery and the like.

Puppies are born blind and don't open their eyes until they are about 10 to 13 days old. The retina is fully developed at about 4 weeks but the part of the brain associated with sight is not fully developed until about 8 weeks of age, although this varies slightly according to breed.

Understanding the importance of visual movement to the dog is one of the keys to being a successful trainer.

Let's look at the training implications related to the sense of sight.

- Puppies may have some difficulty in seeing visual hand signals clearly until they are 8 weeks old.
- Puppies have to learn to locate the direction of sounds such as voice signals so it is better to move away as you call them to help them to locate you at a distance.
- Dogs can discern very subtle changes in hand signals. If more than one person is training a dog, they must try to copy each other's signals accurately, especially during early conditioning, otherwise the dog may become confused.
- Moving hand signals will elicit much more interest than static ones. You can use this to your advantage! That is, use demonstrative hand signals when you want your dog to move with you, such as when you want it to heel beside you (Lesson 7), and avoid hand movements when you want the dog to remain still, for example in the stay exercise (Lesson 5).
- Dogs are very interested in anything which moves close to the ground because prey animals run at this level. Not many dogs are really interested in things happening above their heads. Consequently our hand signals should be given at a low level.
- Dogs are easily stimulated by movement over a wide visual field and may be easily distracted when we want them to pay attention to us! As a result we must give such interesting signals that our dog chooses to respond to *us*.
- Dogs are easily triggered into chasing fast moving things such as joggers, bikes and animals. It is important to condition them not do this at an early age (Lesson 10). Established habits can be hard to break and chasing bikes can be great fun for some dogs!
- At home dogs may bark or try to escape if they see interesting things happening on the other side of the fence. If you try to give your dog a quality lifestyle and have it inside with you most

of the time when you are home, this shouldn't be too much of a problem.

- Excessive facial hair should be clipped or pinned back to allow dogs to see properly. Wolves, dingos, basenjis and other more 'natural' breeds of dog do not have this problem. It wouldn't help them to survive in the wild.
- Dogs may attack fluffy dogs whose body language *appears* to be aggressive. Raising your hair and making yourself look bigger is normally a sign of dominance in dogs. In order to prevent this happening you should socialise your dog with as many breeds of dogs as possible from a very early age.

The Sense of Smell

We marvel at the stories we hear about the dog's incredible sense of smell. On television we can watch them sniffing out people who have been buried in earthquakes or under avalanches, and we hear about them being used to find drugs, gas leaks, and accelerants for burning down buildings illegally. Their sense of smell is estimated to be up to ten million times more efficient than ours. Amazing!

Dogs use this sense to identify one other and to find out important information such as the maturity and sex of another animal and whether it is ready for mating. They can do this by direct scenting or more often by sniffing the other animal's secretions.

The dog's nose extends from the tip of the nostrils to the back of its throat and it has an extra sensory area on the roof of its mouth as well, which is called the vomeronasal organ. The area of nerve receptor cells is said to equal about five times the entire surface of the dog's body! In comparison ours is equal to the size of a postage stamp! No wonder we cannot understand why dogs are so interested in sniffing just about *everything* as they go for a walk!

Smell molecules are easily dissolved in the moisture on the outer surface of the dog's nose. The message is transferred to the brain where it is interpreted by the dog as very interesting, worth investigating or boring! This is why your dog's nose is very moist when you are preparing its food but may feel quite dry when it is asleep. Animals, including humans, tend to smell better when they are hungry.

There are a few substances which are said to repel dogs such as Oil of Citronella and these are used in sprays which are designed to stop dogs from going on certain areas of the garden, for instance. We are a bit sceptical about their effectiveness.

So what implications does this have for training?

- The odour of meat is very stimulating to a dog and should be used when we teach it to do various things, or when we want to modify its behaviour (Chapter 9). If we use our dog's favourite food for training we will increase its motivation to work. Rather like giving us a thousand dollars for a day's work, instead of a hundred!

The Sense of Hearing

Like its other senses, the wolf or dog's hearing is geared to survival. Because wolves are born in a dark den they have their eyes and ear canals closed at birth. Some recent experiments at Wolf Park, Indiana, USA, indicate that wolf cubs may be aware of sounds made by their mother before they are 48 hours old. Their heart rate increased when they heard her. Dogs don't appear to respond to sounds outwardly until they are 18 to 19 days old when their ear canals open. The opening of the ear canals corresponds to the time when the brain and legs are developed well enough to allow the pup to start crawling and exploring outside the immediate den or bed area.

By about 6 weeks the brain has matured to a point where the pup is capable of interpreting sound as well as an adult, but it still has a lot to learn. You will notice that puppies often look around in some bewilderment when you call them. This is because they haven't learnt to pinpoint where the noise is coming from.

Dogs can hear at a much higher level than we can and this is the reason for the use of the so-called 'silent whistle'. This capacity is important for animals which hunt, as some prey species such as rodents make very high squeaky noises and the ability to hear them helps to find food.

Some dogs appear to hear better than others. Probably breeds such as the German Shepherd with its large, erect, mobile ear flaps can hear more efficiently than a Cocker Spaniel with its long pendulous ears. The Cocker Spaniel may compensate with an extraordinary ability to scent. Experiments have shown that dogs can hear distant sounds at least five times better than humans. They can also locate the direction of a sound much more efficiently.

Yet, with all their fantastic ability to hear, dogs do not understand our language as much as we would like to believe. It's not really true when we say 'my dog understands every word I say'. Nevertheless they do home in on sounds which are important to them and are masters at reading our body language. Notice the reaction when you pick up the lead or car keys or when you open the fridge door! They can also learn a great number of *key words,* which makes them *appear* to understand every word we say.

So what implications does this have during training?

• Sounds will not affect puppies to any extent up

Above, the most efficient ears are pricked, but below, this spaniel probably has a better sense of smell.

to 18 to 19 days old. From this time onwards, sound stimuli will affect learning.

• Dogs do not require loud signals as their hearing is better than ours.

• It is better to call a dog in a high pitched voice if you wish to gain its attention. There is no need to 'growl' and in fact this is counter productive. We will explain this in more detail in Chapter 8.

• Dogs may be distracted by noises that a handler cannot hear because of their pitch or volume.

• They will quickly react to noises of personal significance such as food bowls clattering.

• Your dog will pay much less attention to your voice signal if you touch it at the same time (see Touch). It is much better not to distract your dog by touching it, especially during early training.

• Dogs may become agitated or even bite, if air is blown into their faces or ears. It can be dangerous if children are allowed to tease a dog in this way.

• Dogs may be triggered to howl by high pitched noises such as sirens and some music. They may also bark and become excited because of sounds such as children playing and screaming. Your neighbours may not understand this! If you have a problem the obvious solution is to keep your dog indoors with you whenever possible.

• Elderly animals sometimes suffer from a decrease in hearing ability that makes them appear to ignore our voice signals! If you teach your dog to respond to both hand and voice signals during early training it will be simple for it to follow hand signals alone if it becomes deaf. You can also train a deaf puppy with hand signals only, but you will have to make sure that you never get out of its line of sight. If necessary, put it on a long lead.

The Sense of Taste

Some people offer their dogs the same menu year after year but, like us, dogs appreciate some variety. In the wild wolves eat anything from tiny rodents to enormous bison and moose. They are opportunistic feeders and will eat carrion, berries, earth and even the faeces of other animals if food is in short supply. After a kill they consume every part of the carcass including bones, hair, muscle meat and the soft easily consumed internal organs. They find predigested vegetable matter in the stomach and intestine of their victim. We should try to match their natural diet by feeding our animals similar sorts of foodstuffs. Meat, hard, solid bones, pureed vegetables and some extra roughage perhaps in the form of cereal is ideal. Soft food out of a can may be nutritionally well balanced but dogs who are given nothing else can end up with rotten teeth, because they do not have the opportunity to chew, and itchy skin due to the preservatives which are added to artificial food to extend its shelf life. It often seems to give them loose stools as well and this is not very pleasant when you have to dispose of them! Loose stools can also lead to blocked anal ducts.

Our dogs often end up being far too fat so we should also try to emulate the wolf's *frequency* of feeding! Wolves eat enormous quantities of food when they make a kill and then they may go for days without tasting another morsel. Perhaps they may gnaw on a bone if there is one left. In contrast, we tend to feed our dogs at least once a day, sometimes more! On top of that they often have very little exercise and consequently have a low basal metabolic rate. No wonder they stack on the weight! Diet and exercise have to be balanced in any animal, dog or human. We discuss feeding regimes in more detail in Chapter 9.

There isn't a great deal of information about the dog's sense of taste. They'll usually eat anything that smells good, which can include dangerous substances like snail bait.

So what implications does this have during training?

- When training your dog it is a good idea to use food that your dog really likes as a reinforcement. Fresh meat is the natural choice for all canines, and it has the added advantage that it doesn't crumble and drop to the ground like dry food.

The Sense of Touch

'I gave my dog a good pat' is an expression that most dog owners can relate to. When you think about it, physical contact between man and dog is probably more frequent than between man and any other

Dogs don't have the manual dexterity of humans.

animal. But who is *really* benefiting from this type of interaction? If the truth be known, touch is not one of the more important senses in the dog. Wolves do not spend time patting one another for obvious reasons; they do not have hands. Of course, there are numerous instances when they *do* use their sense of touch: scratching the ground, grasping when copulating, carrying food to their mouths, rolling in some smelly substance and mouthing each other. The list is long. However, their primary tactile needs are balance, temperature control and avoidance of pain. *Our* physical contact with dogs is well down on *their* list of survival needs. We find this hard to understand because we use our hands and our sense of touch to carry out thousands of tasks every day and many of us use our manual dexterity to earn our living. It has become a major factor in *our* means of survival.

Some people put great faith in the use of touch, such as patting, as a means of teaching their dog. However, the aim of this book is to explain how we can communicate with our dogs in the *most successful* way. It stands to reason that if dogs do not rely on touch for survival in the wild, then we would be foolish to think that it is suddenly going to have a great influence on them when they are domesticated. Too much credence is given to the value of patting as a means of rewarding dogs.

Unfortunately, some people still use touch in a violent way in an attempt to change their dog's behaviour, for example by jerking it on the neck with a choker chain or hitting it with a rolled up newspaper. We will discuss the implications of these types of punishment in Chapter 8 but anyone who has tried them will have noticed that they lead to cringing or fearful behaviour in some dogs and a tendency to aggression in others. It is easier to understand this if we put ourselves in our dog's paws. For instance, how would we react to a boss who admonished us when we did something he didn't like and then neglected to explain what we had done to upset him? Wouldn't we prefer him to show us what to do correctly and then reward our good behaviour? This will be the subject of the next chapter.

Training implications of the sense of touch:
- Touching a dog during training will cause a distraction, for example touching it on the rump to make it sit may make it whirl around to see what is going on. It is always better to limit the use of touch, such as patting, to a non-training situation.
- The use of touch as a punishment in the compulsive method of training often leads to fear, resentment and avoidance behaviour, especially in more 'sensitive' dogs. Bold dogs may react in an aggressive manner.
- Touch is an inefficient way to reward or reinforce a dog when you compare it with the use of food.

Fun on the farm

Chapter 7

The Gentle Modern Method of Dog Training^{TM pending}

We are very lucky to be able to use the discoveries of modern science to help us train our dogs. In the days before the development of psychology, people relied on the attitude and knowledge that prevailed at the time. Caning children was an acceptable part of the teaching process and, in the same way, dogs were trained mainly by force. It is thought that the first organised training of dogs in groups took place in Germany at the time of the First World War when dogs were taught to run between the trenches carrying messages in pouches strapped around their bodies. The method of training was harsh and demanding. It became known as the compulsive method.

Since then we have discovered a great deal about the way dogs learn. In particular, an American named Skinner, who was a behavioural scientist, conducted experiments with a variety of animals and showed how animals learn, why they remember or forget, what motivates them and how a behaviour is sustained. His findings are as relevant and factual today as they were when he published his first book *The Behaviour of Organisms* in 1938. Today, behavioural science is studied in universities around the world but unfortunately many dog owners have not had the opportunity to find out about this science which would be so useful to them when training their dogs.

Leads attached to a choker chain around a dog's neck make a lethal combination. When the neck is jerked, the dog has to respond, or suffer. Shouted commands, often uttered in a menacing manner, are designed to harass and intimidate. A cowering dog with lowered head, ears and tail is often the end product of a harsh training method used by the handler. Alternatively, a dominant dog may resent the punishment and eventually attack the handler or it may displace its aggression and bite an innocent bystander. This method and attitude still prevails in many places today. If you think we are exaggerating, talk to someone whose dog has been damaged by these techniques.

Conditioning—The Natural Way of Learning

It may be a little hard to understand that dogs can be trained without using a lead and even without touching them. Most people can't imagine how they can get a dog to lie down, sit or heel beside them without controlling it with a choker chain or pushing its bottom onto the ground.

The method of training which David developed

back in the mid 1960s doesn't make demands on the dog to do anything. The dog makes the choice of what *it* wants to do. Its responses are entirely voluntary. Put it this way. If a dog finds a certain behaviour is beneficial, it will be more likely to repeat it and, if it finds no benefit, it is unlikely to pursue it. Sounds simple doesn't it? And so it is, if you know how to go about motivating and reinforcing a dog in the most meaningful way.

Most people know that dogs of any breed are descended from wolves. The following description illustrates how a wolf cub learns naturally. Imagine it wandering out of its den and investigating its surroundings. Suddenly its sense of sight is stimulated by the movement of a small rodent running across the ground. Its sense of hearing picks up a rustling sound. Its sense of smell detects an odour. It responds to these stimuli by chasing the rodent and killing it. The cub is reinforced by getting something to eat. It is natural that if similar sights and sounds occur again that the cub will respond in the same way as before. Voila! learning has taken place. In fact we all follow this pattern. We tend to repeat things that we find beneficial or *reinforcing* and avoid things which we do not like! We can use the same natural learning process to train our domestic dogs.

Reinforcement—How we 'Strengthen' Behaviour

The use of food

Of course you can't use a rodent as your stimulus, but you can substitute others, such as the voice signal 'come' and a hand signal, for example putting your hand down low to the ground with a piece of food in it. Your dog will want to move towards your hand to investigate it. If you reinforce this behaviour by giving your dog a piece of food when it comes to you, it will tend to come to you more and more predictably each time it hears the word 'come' and sees the same hand signal.

Some people are worried when we give this explanation because they think it means they will have to carry a bucket of food with them for ever more! It doesn't work that way! *After a few repetitions of the same stimulus, response and reinforcement, the dog will become* <u>*conditioned*</u> *to respond to the voice and hand signal and will only need to be reinforced occasionally.* Other people are worried because they feel that using food to train a dog is tantamount to bribery and they have been told that: 'Your dog should respond to you out of respect' or 'Your dog should respond because it loves you'. Then there are the dog owners who are under the impression that the dog will stop responding if there is no food available. Nothing is further from the truth.

We often try to explain about the power of reinforcement by drawing an analogy with human behaviour, for example a lady playing a poker machine. She keeps putting money in the machine and pulling the handle in the hope that she will receive a reinforcement in the form of winning lots of money! Gambling machines are programmed to deliver intermittent reinforcement and so they keep people trying over and over again. The occasional win sustains the habit! You may be aware that the government is spending millions of dollars every year to help people break the powerful gambling habit; *such is the power of intermittent reinforcement!*

When we train dogs it is very important to understand this pattern of *random reinforcement*.

The use of patting as a reinforcement

A lot of people who train dogs use patting to reinforce a behaviour.

We have found that patting is an inefficient way to sustain a behaviour compared with the use of food. For example, if I placed your dog between us and every time you called your dog you patted it, and every time I called your dog I fed it, who do you think your dog would choose to come to more often? You're right, your dog would respond to me! So when we look at the difference in efficiency of reinforcers, that is of food versus patting, we can clearly see that food is more beneficial.

Other reinforcers

This is not to say that other things cannot be used as reinforcers. Some dogs are fanatical retrievers and the opportunity to chase and fetch a ball may be highly reinforcing for them. However, such reinforcers can also make the dog very excitable and this can lead to problems. It is also more difficult to teach a dog conventional exercises using a ball alone.

Shaping Behaviour

Food is used in two ways when we are training. As well as using it as a reinforcement we use it to *shape behaviour*.

When we are teaching a new exercise, we use food in our hand as an extra stimulus in order to get the dog into the position we want. In other words we *shape* the behaviour we wish to produce. Then, when the dog responds in the way we desire, we reinforce that response by giving it the piece of food. Initially we reinforce the dog after nearly every response, as shown in Diagram 1 below.

If we didn't shape the dog's actions we would have to wait until the dog spontaneously took up the position we wanted, for example sitting, before we could reinforce it, and that could take ages! Or we would have to manhandle it into the sit position by pushing its bottom down onto the ground. This isn't a good idea because the use of force will cause resentment and unwilling responses.

The hand movements we use to shape a dog's behaviour are unique to the Gentle Modern Method and took some years for David to perfect.

Let's look at just one example of shaping a new behaviour, for example teaching your dog to sit in front of you.

Diagram 1 Teaching a New Exercise

Food in the hand as an inducement
(Unconditioned stimulus)

Hand signal and Voice signal, 'Sit'
(Neutral stimuli which become conditioned)

The dog sits in response to the movement of the food in the hand
(Unconditioned response)

Food is given to the dog
(Reinforcement)

After several pairings of food inducement with the hand and voice signals the dog will learn to respond to the hand and voice signals only.
(i.e. Conditioned response)

46

The technical terms in brackets are explained in Chapter 9, so you may want to come back and look at Diagrams 1 and 2 when you have finished reading that chapter.

When a dog has learnt an exercise, usually when it has done it about six to ten times, then you *must* stop carrying food in the hand as part of the signal and start to give the dog food *intermittently after* it has responded. *It's important that your hand signals remain the same* whether you have food in your hand or not. This is illustrated in Diagram 2.

The next chapter explains the theory behind the Gentle Modern Training Method. The information it contains will be useful for people who have not got a qualified instructor nearby and who want to use this method to train their dogs, and for anyone who is interested in finding out more about how animals learn.

The Australian Association of Gentle Modern Dog Training Instructors Inc.

This Association has been formed to provide support and training for dog training clubs and instructors who would like to teach courses using The Gentle Modern Method of Dog Training. Further information can be obtained from Ruth Weston, 8 Sackville Street, Montmorency, Victoria 3094, telephone/fax (03) 9439 8546.

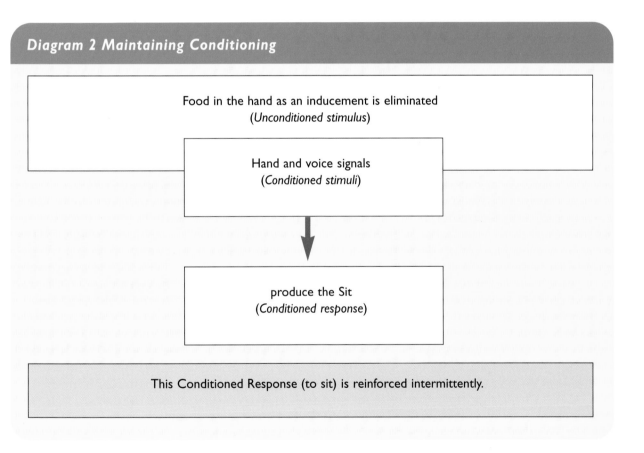

Diagram 2 Maintaining Conditioning

Food in the hand as an inducement is eliminated
(*Unconditioned stimulus*)

Hand and voice signals
(*Conditioned stimuli*)

produce the Sit
(*Conditioned response*)

This Conditioned Response (to sit) is reinforced intermittently.

Chapter 8

How Dogs Learn—
The Theory

Animals learn in a number of ways but mostly by what is called *classical* and *operant* conditioning. In our training method we use a combination of these two techniques. The first was discovered almost by accident by Ivan Pavlov and the second was perfected by Professor Skinner who was mentioned in the last chapter.

Dogs will learn whether you make a deliberate attempt to teach them or not! So why not teach your dog what *you* want it to learn! The secret of how to train your dog really effectively is to have a sound knowledge about conditioning. There are a few technical terms you must know.

A stimulus = Anything which will generate a response.

A response = Anything which occurs as the result of a stimulus.

Behaviour = Any response to a stimulus.

Learning = Modification to behaviour which is usually based on past experience.

Classical Conditioning

In the early part of the twentieth century the Russian physiologist Pavlov was studying digestion in dogs by connecting a tube to one of the salivary glands in their mouths and seeing what happened when food was offered. After he had conducted a few trials he found that his experiments were being distorted because the dogs started to salivate when they heard the sound of food being prepared or the footsteps of the staff bringing them food.

He decided to study this phenomenon and find out what would happen if he made all sorts of noises before he offered the dogs food. To his amazement, he found that whatever sound he produced, whether it was the sound of a metronome, bell or tuning fork, it would still cause the dogs to salivate if the sound was followed by them being fed. Next he tried making the sound without offering food. He discovered that the dogs continued to salivate even when food was not given to them afterwards. However, this salivation response did not continue indefinitely if food never followed.

Pavlov's discovery, which was named classical conditioning, is concerned with *involuntary* responses, or reflexes, over which the dog has *no control* , e.g. salivation in response to food, or blinking when air is puffed into the eye. No reward, or reinforcement, is required.

1 The dog hears the sound of a tuning fork. (A neutral stimulus)

2 The dog is then given meat. (An unconditioned stimulus)

3 The dog salivates in response *to the meat*. (An unconditioned response)

4 1, 2 and 3 are repeated a number of times.

5 The dog hears the sound of the tuning fork but is given no meat. (At this stage the neutral stimulus has become a conditioned stimulus.)

6 The result is that the dog salivates *to the sound*. (A conditioned response)

Operant Conditioning

Skinner, following on the work of early behaviourists such as Watson, Thorndike and Hull, studied the effects of reinforcement and punishment and developed a learning theory which he called operant conditioning. The process emphasised the power of reinforcement as a way of influencing behaviour. We would like to see everyone involved in dog training using positive reinforcement, because it is the most powerful technique we have at our disposal for directing or motivating the actions of animals.

Reinforcement

A *reinforcement* is anything which benefits the dog and therefore creates, or maintains a behaviour. There are two main types of reinforcers, positive and negative:

1 *Positive reinforcement increases the frequency of the dog's response* when a reinforcement is given immediately after a response, e.g. the dog is *given food after sitting on signal.*

Positive reinforcers can be further broken down into two sub types:

(a) An **unconditioned, or primary reinforcer** is a reinforcer which has immediate biological importance to the animal, e.g. food, water, sex. Unconditioned or primary reinforcers are essential for survival.

(b) A **conditioned, or secondary reinforcer** comes to act as a reinforcer because it is paired with an unconditioned or primary reinforcer, e.g. giving the dog food and praising it at the same time will make praise reinforcing in its own right. It is very important to realise that the durability of conditioned or secondary reinforcers is poor if they are not occasionally paired with unconditioned or primary

reinforcers. *They NEVER achieve the powerful control over behaviour that primary reinforcers do.*

2 *Negative reinforcement increases the frequency of a dog's response* when a punishment (aversive event) is *removed or stopped* immediately after the response. You cannot use negative reinforcement unless you are prepared to subject your dog to something unpleasant first. Punishment and negative reinforcement are the techniques used by dog handlers who practise the compulsive method of training, e.g. the dog heels at the handler's side and the handler *stops jerking the dog in the neck with a choke chain (a negative reinforcement).*

Operant conditioning is concerned with **voluntary** responses over which the dog *does* have control, i.e if a response is seen to be beneficial it will be repeated, and if the response is not beneficial it will not be repeated.

The advantages of using positive reinforcement as a teaching technique in dog training

1 It's a natural learning process using the dog's most important senses.

2 It develops an excellent relationship between the handler and dog.

3 It produces a bold, outgoing attitude on the part of the dog.

4 It makes the dog eager to learn.

5 Numerous responses can be taught starting at a very young age.

6 The retention of a learnt behaviour will last indefinitely as long as it is reinforced occasionally.

Punishment and negative reinforcement

A **punishment** is any sort of aversive event which is generally damaging, painful or simply uncomfortable for the animal, e.g. the use of a choke chain. *Punishment is a technique designed to stop a behaviour.* However, punishment must be *severe* if it is going to be effective, and it must be given *immediately* after the undesirable response. It has numerous disadvantages and undesirable consequences.

1 The behaviour produced is **involuntary** behaviour. Think how you would react if someone repeatedly *made* you do things against your will!

2 Moderate degrees of punishment and negative reinforcement will produce learning after a *considerable* number of repetitions. Do we really

want to be so inefficient and achieve results in a draconian manner?

3 The severity of punishment has to be gradually increased to sustain the response. Dogs are our best friends. Say no more.

4 Some dogs will react to punishment by becoming fearful and their fear will make them unwilling, or unable to learn. This is self defeating.

5 More 'dominant' or 'superior' dogs may react to punishment by becoming aggressive. They may bite but are more likely to bite someone other than their owner.

6 When a person punishes a dog it destroys the social relationship between the dog and that person. The dog will probably learn to be either nervous or aggressive towards everyone depending on its temperament.

As Professor Skinner said in one of the last written statements prior to his death: 'Anyone who remains satisfied with punishment without exploring non-punitive alternatives is making a real mistake.'

Extinction

This is the process of consistently withholding a reinforcement after responses which have been reinforced in the past, for example a dog handler reinforces a dog every time it sits for a while and then stops doing this completely. This will result in the dog sitting less and less frequently until it ultimately stops responding altogether. I think you would do the same if you went to work and no one paid you over a long period of time! It is called extinction simply because the response has been extinguished.

The more predictable you are when you offer reinforcement during training, the more rapidly the dog will cease to respond when reinforcement is withheld. It is very important to start introducing intermittent reinforcement *very early* in your training if you want to be a successful dog trainer. If you do this your dog will not be able to predict when it is going to be reinforced and it will keep responding indefinitely. Remember the poker machine?!

Extinction is a useful tool in modifying dog behaviour, e.g. if you *never* reinforce a dog for begging at the table again, the begging behaviour will go into extinction.

A detailed example of teaching a basic exercise using positive reinforcement is given at the end of Lesson 1.

Preparing for Training

Good teachers try to organise ideal conditions for learning in their classrooms. They motivate their students to do well, communicate with them effectively and actively reinforce good work. We can do the same with our dogs. Training should not be regarded as separate from ordinary life. When your dog has learnt a lesson it is quite all right to practice it when you are out walking or in the midst of household activities. This will teach your dog to respond under all sorts of different conditions. However, new lessons are best learnt in a place where there are no distractions.

Here is a checklist which will help you to prepare for training wherever you are.

1 Try to cut out any distractions, e.g. noisy children and other animals, *during early training* until your dog is conditioned.

2 Arrange any equipment you need for the exercises which you are going to teach *before you start.*

3 Prepare tasty reinforcements for your dog. Small chunks of fresh meat such as a stewing steak are usually the best. Forty pieces should be sufficient. Avoid using any food which crumbles, otherwise your dog may spend half its time vacuuming the ground! You can keep the food in a pouch tied round your waist if you wish or put it in a plastic bag in your pocket out of sight of the dog.

4 Train your dog *when it is very keen for food*, i.e. before a mealtime, so that it is motivated to earn its reinforcements.

If your dog does not have a naturally keen appetite then we strongly suggest that you feed it every 36 hours for a week or two instead of every 24, unless your veterinarian has advised you to feed your dog frequently because it has a specific medical problem. You can increase the quantity of food given at each meal so that your dog actually consumes the usual number of calories per week—it just eats less often. The dog's appetite should improve fairly rapidly because it is hungry when each meal is offered. We strongly recommend that you don't leave food in your dog's dish for more than 15 minutes. If it has not eaten it by then, it's not hungry! Take the food away and don't offer anything else until the next scheduled meal. This includes bones, milk and titbits!

There are some dog welfare organisations whose code of ethics stipulates that dogs should be fed every 24 hours and young dogs under 6 months should be fed twice a day. This is probably because they have seen some horrendous cases of neglect where dogs have been literally starved to death, and they want to educate people to feed their dogs regularly. However, anyone who is reading this book obviously cares for their dog and is not going to starve it!

It is actually natural for wolves to go for 4 or 5 days without eating and they may use a great deal of energy hunting vigorously during this period. Then they really tuck in and eat a great deal, sometimes as much as 8 kilos (18 pounds) each. Your dog has the same kind of digestive system as the wolf! Sometimes we do our dogs a disservice by feeding them every 24 hours so that they become sluggish and obese! Dogs should 'wolf' their food down; if they are picky eaters there is something wrong either with their health or the schedule of feeding.

Young puppies should be fed about three times a day from 8 to 10 weeks of age. Most pups require two meals a day between 10 and 14 weeks and one meal a day thereafter. This will encourage healthy eating habits. An underweight puppy should continue on two meals a day for longer.

We are not going to attempt to give you very much information about nutrition because it is not within the scope of this book. Suffice to say that we believe that you should try to mimic the dog's natural diet rather than feeding it soft commercial dog food. Meat, sturdy bones, pureed vegetables, and some roughage like bran, rice or pasta are all ideal. Eggs, filleted fish and cheese can be used as alternative sources of protein. There are many good books on dog nutrition which will offer more comprehensive information.

If your dog appears to be unwell or is underweight see your veterinarian for advice. You should let a sick dog rest and not try to train it until it has recovered. It may need small meals more often during the recovery phase.

Remember that food is the easiest and most efficient form of reinforcement for any dog with natural eating habits.

5 When you offer food in the form of a reinforcement, make sure that you do so in a positive way by presenting your hand straight to your dog's mouth. Some people put their hand out in a rather tentative fashion and then withdraw it as the dog's mouth comes close to their fingers. This will only encourage the dog to snatch at the food and you may inadvertently get bitten.

You can discourage dogs who grab at food in the hand by offering it in a clenched fist and then opening your hand to reveal the food. This simply creates a delay.

6 Your clothes should be suitable for training. Dogs seem to be distracted by rubber boots or sandals that flop up and down. Avoid wearing skirts or coats which billow out at the dog's eye level so that it can't see your signals. Slacks, lace-up shoes and a T-shirt or jumper are probably best. A short rain jacket can be used if necessary, but who wants to train in the rain anyway?!

Offering food to your dog: a clenched fist discourages the grabbers.

7 Make sure you understand the principles of operant conditioning which we discussed in Chapters 7 and 8.

8 It is a good idea to practise your hand signals in front of a mirror to see if you are doing them correctly before you teach your dog. David did this for hours when he was developing this method of training!

9 Stimulate your dog by using its senses in the most meaningful way *to the dog,*—see Chapter 6. The main things to remember are:

  • Dogs hear better at a higher level so call your dog in a high pitched voice.
  • Keep your voice signals quiet so that they don't sound threatening to your dog. A fearful dog can't learn. Both you and your dog should always enjoy training.
  • Your dog is easily stimulated by moving hand signals at ground level.
  • Your dog will respond much more readily to hand signals than voice signals.

10 Obviously your dog should be fit and healthy for training and you should have enough time to enjoy yourselves in a leisurely fashion.

Working and playing with your dog is fun.

Training should always be a pleasure.

Fun after training

PART 2
The Lessons

How to Train Your Ideal Dog

How to Use this Book when Teaching Lessons I to I4

You will be required to teach your dog most, if not all, the lessons in this book in order to pass the training assessments in various countries as the requirements differ very little from country to country. These lessons have been planned so that *all* the skills required for *all* the assessments are covered but we suggest that, even if you don't need some of them, it will help you and your dog to become even more perfect if you teach them all. A coloured section at the start of each chapter indicates which exercises are required for each country's assessment. A check means that you must teach your dog the exercise in order to pass the assessment.

Australia	✔
Victoria	✔
WA	✔
UK	✔
USA	✔

Ideal Dogs of Australia is colour coded in yellow, Victoria's Approved Dog Obedience Assessment Program is in green, The Canine Association of Western Australia's Canine Good Companion Programme is colour coded in purple. The American Kennel Club's Canine Good Citizen Test is in light blue and The UK Kennel Club's Good Citizen Dog Scheme is in orange. As far as we know these countries and Japan are the only ones so far which have introduced short training courses specifically designed to teach dogs to be well behaved members of the community. As we hear of other countries coming into the movement we will include them in our colour coding. The full assessment criteria are reprinted in an Appendix at the end of this book by kind permission of the organisations concerned, and we have added references to the exercises you will need to teach to pass each section.

The exercises are presented in a logical sequence and we recommend that you teach them in roughly the same order.

Sometimes a number of exercises must be combined in order to complete one part of an assessment, for example walking on a loose lead requires your dog to learn to heel, sit, drop and to do all types of turns.

Obedience classes in the Rocky Mountains
© Kent and Donna Dannen

Canine Good Citizens

Sharing

All photographs in this section © Kent & Donna Dannen

Caring

Australia	✓
Victoria	✓
WA	✓
UK	✓
USA	✓

The Recall

Why should an Ideal Dog Come when Called?

This is the most important exercise you will ever teach your dog. How many times have you heard a person calling their dog in a rather exasperated way while it simply ignores them, and often moves off in the opposite direction! The consequences can be devastating. An uncontrolled dog may run onto the road and end up getting killed or injured, or even cause a traffic accident leading to loss of life.

What does the dog owner do? Unfortunately many of the most common solutions to this problem can make the situation even worse. Sometimes owners stop taking their dog out for walks and confine it to the backyard where it becomes bored, barks and gets into mischief. Other people still take their dog out but keep it on a lead even in open park areas. They often create additional problems for themselves such as inadvertently teaching their dog to pull madly on the lead because it wants to do normal doggy things like sniffing, running, and meeting other dogs, and the lead prevents it from doing so. Further behavioural problems may develop due to lack of exercise and boredom. The owner may end up by having the dog 'put down'.

How much simpler it is to teach your dog to respond to you even when there are exciting distractions around. This is very easy provided you use the teaching technique of positive reinforcement.

Remember, however, that dogs are masters at reading body language! If your dog has already developed the problem of not coming back when it's called, and you have been showing annoyance when it eventually did return, then you have not been giving it any reason to *want* to come to you in the future. Needless to say punishing your dog for coming to you would be totally unproductive.

Teaching the Lesson

If your dog has developed the habit of not coming when it is called, or if it 'comes when it chooses', it is important to start off by practising this exercise in a confined area. In addition, your dog must be truly keen for food, see Chapter 9. We suggest that you start by practising in your house without distractions, gradually building up to working outside in the garden, and finally in a more open area where dogs are allowed off lead. Never allow your dog to run free on, or close to a road however well trained it is.

Prepare your dog for training as shown in Chapter 9.

1 Wait until your dog is looking at you from a short distance away.

2 Move away from your dog to encourage it to come towards you, and drop either your right or left hand low to the ground. At this stage your hand should have food in it.

3 Say 'Come' *once only* when your dog is actually moving towards you and you are positive that you are going to produce the desired response.

4 Reinforce your dog with the piece of food in your hand the moment it reaches you.

5 Remove your hand quickly away up to waist level.

6 Repeat points 1 to 5 until your dog's behaviour becomes predictable, i.e. conditioned. This will take about 6 to 10 repetitions.

NOTE: Never say the word 'Come' when your dog is running *away* from you during *early training*, otherwise your dog will fail to make the connection between the word 'Come' and the act of running *towards* you. Simply say your dog's name and, when it looks at you and moves towards you, then call 'Come' as described above.

Maintaining your Dog's Response

Once your dog's response is predictable and it always comes to you on signal you should do the following to maintain its response:

1 Stop using food in your hand to help stimulate a response.

2 The hand signal *must remain the same* whether there is food in your hand or not. Dogs can detect very subtle variations in hand signals.

3 You should not need to move away from your dog unless it is responding slowly.

4 The food you are using as a reinforcement should be kept in a pocket or pouch where it is not obvious to your dog.

5 Start to reinforce your dog *intermittently* so that it cannot predict when it will be fed. Don't make the intervals between reinforcers too long to begin with, e.g. reinforce the second, fifth, and third responses, always choosing the 'best' responses to reinforce.

The difference between teaching the exercise and maintaining your dog's response (see Chapters 7 and 8) should now be clear. See the Table below:

Teaching the exercise	Maintaining your dog's response
The Stimulus	*The Stimulus*
• Your movement away from your dog. • Your hand signal low to the ground. • Your voice signal 'Come'. • The food in your hand.	• Your hand signal low to the ground. • Your voice signal 'Come'.
The Response	*The Response*
The dog is *induced* to come in response to the above stimuli.	The dog *comes* in response to the above stimuli.
The Reinforcement	*The Reinforcement*
The food is given from your hand after every successful response.	The food is given **intermittently** from your pocket.

Lesson 2

Sit on Signal

Why should an Ideal Dog Sit on Signal?

The sit is an extremely useful exercise in our society. When your dog sits on signal it is automatically less threatening to other people and, in fact, it is impossible for it to jump up on people if its bottom is firmly on the ground!

The sit is also needed as an introduction to many other useful canine skills such as staying, putting on a lead, waiting for a meal, and so on.

Teaching the Lessons

A. Sit in front

It is easier to teach your dog to sit in front of you before teaching it to sit at your left-hand side.

| Call your dog. As it approaches you, place your hand containing food at your dog's nose level.

2 Draw your hand in a flowing motion towards your legs and then up to approximately waist level, bringing your body upright at the same time. This will cause your dog to look up and fall into the sit position.

3 Say 'Sit' *once only* as your dog starts to adopt the sit position.

4 Reinforce your dog with food from your hand the moment its bottom reaches the ground.

5 Remove your hand quickly back to its original position at waist level.

6 Repeat points 1 to 5 until your dog's response becomes predictable.

NOTE: If your signals do not produce the desired response, it is important for you to check your own actions and timing, e.g. was your signal too fast for the dog to follow or did you stay bent over your dog like a banana? This can make a dog feel crowded causing it to back away from you.

Jumping up!

We often unwittingly teach our dogs to jump up on us because we reinforce them for doing so! It is so difficult not to reward the greeting of that cute little puppy by giving it a pat and a cuddle! However, we're unlikely to appreciate the same behaviour from a fully grown, muddy adult dog! The answer is to be consistent and not reinforce this type of behaviour in the first place.

You can use the sit exercise very effectively to modify your dog's behaviour if it does have an established jumping up problem. You must time your signals so that you generate the sit response *before your dog thinks about jumping!* Your friends can be taught to do the same thing or they can be given a piece of food and asked to reinforce the dog in the stand position (see Lesson 3).

B. Sit at the left-hand side

This is basically the same exercise as the Sit in Front except that the dog is on your left side and consequently your hand movements are made at your left side.

In this position your dog is less likely to jump up, will accept patting more readily and generally be calmer. It is a good starting position for heeling.

1 Call your dog to your left-hand side by placing your right hand, containing food, across your body and drawing your dog into a stand position beside you. Its head should be in line with the tips of your shoes.

2 Raise this hand upwards in a flowing motion to approximately waist level *directly* above your dog's head. Your dog will look up and fall into the sit position.

3 Say 'Sit' *once only* as soon as it starts to adopt the sit position.

4 Reinforce the dog with the food from your hand the moment its bottom touches the ground.

5 Repeat points 1 to 4 until the dog's behaviour becomes predictable.

NOTE: If your dog is very tall or you are short, you may have to raise your hand higher than waist level.

Maintaining Your Dog's Response

Use the same technique as we explained for the Recall, Lesson 1. That is, stop using food in your hand to induce the sit action, and reinforce your dog *intermittently* when it sits rapidly in response to *one* hand and voice signal. Never reinforce a slow or unenthusiastic response.

'My sort of weather'

Lesson 3

Stand on Signal

Why should an Ideal Dog Stand on Signal?

When your dog can stand on signal, it can easily be groomed, petted or examined by a veterinary surgeon. Teaching your dog to stand is also useful when heeling, meeting other dogs, etc. These lessons are required for your dog to earn a certificate and they are all extremely useful in daily life.

Teaching *the Lesson*

1 Sit your dog at your left-hand side, see Lesson 2.

2 Place your right hand containing food immediately in front of your dog's nose.

3 Take a small step forward with your left leg, simultaneously moving your right hand forward and drawing your dog into the stand position. Say 'Stand' the moment the dog starts to adopt the stand position.

4 Feed the dog immediately after it stands, then remove your hand promptly. Draw your hand away at the dog's *nose level* so that it does not see your hand going upwards, otherwise it will tend to interpret your hand movement as a sit signal.

5 Allow your dog to remain in the stand for a few seconds before signalling it to change position. It is a good idea to reinforce your dog a few times in the stand position before it thinks of moving. You can do this by taking 2 or 3 pieces of food in your right hand, then reinforcing with 1 piece, withdrawing your hand, reinforcing it again quickly, and so on.

6 Repeat points 1 to 5 a few times. Do not repeat the sequence 'sit, stand, sit, stand' too frequently or your dog may begin to anticipate the sit signal and sit before you ask it to.

Maintaining Your Dog's Response

Do this as in previous lessons by eliminating food in your hand as a stimulus or inducement, and *intermittently* reinforcing your dog's response to the stand signal.

Lesson 4

Drop on Signal

Why should an Ideal Dog Drop on Signal?

When a dog is lying down it conveys a calm and restful image. There must be millions of photographs of dogs curled up beside their owners' feet or just leaning against their legs. When there 'ain't nuthin' else to do' quiet dogs just plonk themselves down, but not all dogs are like this. Some dogs are bred to be active most of their waking lives. For instance, herding breeds need little goading to race around and this can intimidate some people.

Some dogs are born to be restless but others are made restless by their owners. Dogs can easily be hyped up by endless games of ball or stick throwing. Car or bike chasers were probably quiet little pups once. Playing with your dog by pushing it away so that it bounces back at you will also generate wilder and wilder responses.

However, no matter what breed your dog is or what lifestyle it has, it will lie down and be passive at some stage. If you can teach your dog to adopt the prone position on signal it will definitely help to produce a calmer dog.

Teaching the Lesson

1 Place your dog in a sit position beside your left leg.

2 Bring your right hand containing food to a point just slightly above your dog's nose.

3 Take a short step forward with your left leg and, at the same time, move your right hand past your dog's nose and obliquely down towards the ground in front of your dog's paws.

4 Turn the palm of your right hand down as you do this, so that the food is between you and the ground. Obviously you will have to bend your knees to get your hand into this position.

5 Say 'Drop' as soon as your dog starts to extend its legs forward.

6 Feed the dog immediately after it lies down.

7 Move your hand quickly out of sight keeping it low to the ground until you can bring it up beside the right-hand side of your body without the dog seeing it. Stand upright at the same time.

8 Bring your dog back into the sit position and practise points 1 to 7 a few times, gradually making your hand signal faster.

NOTE: It is sometimes a little difficult to induce a dog with long limbs to lie down, and you may need to reinforce the dog for *starting* to move into the drop position. Get the dog to move further down each time before reinforcing it. The technical term for this technique is '*reinforcing approximations*'.

Maintaining your Dog's Response

Do this in the usual way by eliminating food in your hand as a stimulus and reinforcing the drop response intermittently.

Australia	✓
Victoria	✓
WA	✓
UK	✓
USA	✓

Stay Still on Signal

Why should an Ideal Dog Stay Still on Signal?

The Stay is an important part of a dog's education, mainly because when we teach this exercise we also reinforce passive behaviour. Obviously this is a particularly useful exercise for very active dogs. There are numerous benefits: a dog is less threatening to others when it is still, rather than leaping around, and it can be groomed more easily or medically examined (Lesson 6). Also you can use the Stay exercise to teach your dog not to chase things like bicycles, cats and the fast moving objects which often trigger the hunt chase response in dogs (Lesson 10).

It is essential to teach your dog to wait quietly while you open the front door of your house or the car door (Lesson 13), and only move out on signal. This can mean the difference between life and death if your front door opens onto the street, or you have to change a tyre on a busy highway.

The word 'Stay' should be used only if you want

Staying en famille

your dog to remain in one position until you return to it. It is advisable to avoid using this word when you are grooming your dog, for instance, or when the vet is examining it, because your dog is unlikely to remain completely still under these circumstances and if it moves you will be 'untraining' it rather than 'training' it. You can substitute some other word such as 'Wait' for these situations.

People often tell their dog to 'Stay' when they leave home to go to work. Do they really want their dog to stay in that one spot until they get home?!

We would advise you to start to teach the Stay when your dog is either sitting or lying down because it has to make more effort to move from these positions. This will give you more opportunity to anticipate any movement and return to your dog *before* it occurs. Remember your dog will learn with maximum efficiency if *you* ensure that it does the exercise correctly so that you can reinforce appropriate behaviour. If you build up the Stay exercise slowly so that the dog never breaks from the desired position then you will progress by leaps and bounds in the long run.

Teaching the Lessons

A. The Sit Stay

Work in an environment without any distractions to start with.

1 Place your dog in a sit position beside your left leg.

2 Say 'Stay' and then reinforce your dog for remaining still in the sit position. Repeat this a few times if your dog seems restless.

3 Next say 'Stay' then step forward a pace with your right foot keeping the left leg, which is closest to the dog, stationary. *Do not use a hand signal at this stage or you may encourage your dog to move forward.*

4 Before the dog attempts to move, return to your *original* position beside it and reinforce it with a piece of food.

5 Gradually increase the distance you move away from your dog to 1 full pace, then 2, 3, etc. Always return back to your *original* position before you offer a reinforcement.

6 When you can move about 3 paces away, turn and face your dog, then return and reinforce it intermittently.

7 You should practice moving out from your dog in different directions so that the dog learns to stay wherever you go. Be careful to build up the exercise slowly when you start moving behind your dog as it is likely to twist around to watch you and could move from position.

Treat each new direction like a new exercise and reinforce your dog continuously for a few responses and then start to reinforce intermittently.

NOTE: Once you have conditioned your dog to stay, you can then introduce a stay hand signal. Place your right hand in front of the dog's eyes as you say the word 'Stay.' Make sure that you return your hand to your right-hand side *before* you step off to leave the dog.

B. The Drop Stay

The Drop Stay is taught in the same way as the Sit Stay. Usually it is easier to teach than the Sit Stay because when a dog is lying down it is more likely to be relaxed and want to stay still. Also, you can leave a piece of dry food between the dog's paws before you leave it so that it is busy eating while you move away. This helps to produce a desirable response, i.e. the dog staying, but you wouldn't want to keep up this form of food inducement for very long! Some dogs are reluctant to lie down on wet, cold ground and, as the assessments in Australia and the USA don't require the dog to stay in the drop position specifically, people living in these countries don't have to worry about this. Just do a Sit Stay instead. UK residents can try to choose a dry piece of ground if their dog dislikes the wet.

C. The Stand Stay

This is undoubtedly the most difficult Stay as the dog is much more likely to move from its position. You can minimise the likelihood of this happening by standing your dog up a slight slope or putting its front feet up on a mat. This usually makes dogs stretch out their back legs and lean forward to maintain their centre of gravity. Your dog must be capable of standing still for an extended period *before* you attempt to move away.

Follow the teaching procedure used for the other Stays but be particularly careful that you do not move your hands around except when you reinforce your dog. If you teach the Sit and Drop Stays first, the dog should learn the Stand Stay very quickly because it already knows what 'Stay' means.

Teaching your Dog to Stay when you are Out of Sight

Although this is not a requirement of any of the assessments, you may want to practise it as it will teach your dog not to be stressed when you leave it for brief periods. It will also help it learn to accept being tied up or left with a stranger for the 'supervised separation', which *is* part of the assessment requirements (Lesson 11).

8 Continue to practise point 7, getting further away all the time. Then go out of sight for a very short time perhaps by walking around a car or a tree, then return and reinforce your dog. Very gradually extend the time you are out of the dog's sight, following the principle of progressing slowly so that you are always successful.

NOTE: You will need an assistant to tell you if your dog moves when you go out of sight, or you may be able to watch the dog through a peephole. Remember never to reinforce your dog for moving from position. Dogs which have been left in a drop position have been known to sit up, then lie down again on the same spot, and it is important not to reinforce such a response. Remember to reinforce *intermittently* once your dog is conditioned.

There are a few dogs who become excessively worried when their handler goes out of sight. You can help these dogs to become accustomed to this exercise if you ask a friend whom the dog knows and likes to go and reinforce it while you are away.

If your dog moves from its position when you are out of sight, it is probably better to ask a friend to go and put it back in its original position so that it does not learn that by moving it can make you re-appear.

Maintaining your Dog's Response

Do this in the usual way by eliminating food as an inducement and reinforcing the correct responses intermittently. We will presume in future lessons that our pattern of teaching is now clear and that you no longer need reminders about what to do once your dog has *learnt* the exercise.

Staying quietly with the family

Lesson 6

Enjoying Being Touched

Why should an Ideal Dog

A. *Sit politely while it's patted*
   Accept a friendly stranger
   React calmly to another dog
B. *Be able to be groomed*
C. *Accept a veterinary examination?*

These requirements of the various assessments are all concerned with teaching your dog to enjoy being touched. We have grouped them together because there is a great similarity about how to teach them.

A dog that welcomes a pat is a boon to all dog owners. It is a great public relations exercise if your dog can be touched by young children without bouncing around and knocking them over or, worse still, growling or showing resentment. Adults love to stroke dogs, too. We feel good when we see that a dog wants to be friends with us. People who are rather nervous about dogs often change their attitude dramatically when they meet a number of friendly dogs, especially puppies which tend to be less threatening.

Obviously it is important for dogs to react well to other dogs and learn to stay calm when they are around. Then walking your dog becomes a truly relaxing recreation and you can talk to other dog owners without fuss. In short, a friendly dog is a great social asset.

The benefits of pet therapy are now very widely accepted and dogs visit homes and hospitals in many parts of the world to help make the surroundings more natural and normal. When dogs are used for pet therapy it is particularly important that they are conditioned to accept touching which is not always as gentle as it might be! Therapy dogs must also be conditioned to sudden uncontrolled movements, unusual sounds, and to the movement of sticks, frames and wheelchairs (see Lesson 10). For this reason, they must have bold temperaments and be extremely well socialised from an early age. A fearful dog may be triggered to bite in an out-of-the-ordinary situation.

Pet therapy

74

A. Sitting politely while it's patted
Accepting a friendly stranger
Reacting calmly to another dog
Meeting another person and patting each other's dogs

These exercises can be taught on or off lead according to the test requirements in your country. However, when you are teaching your dog using the Gentle Modern Method we recommend that you work without a lead, at least at first, so that there is no temptation to use it as an aversive training aid. The dog should learn to accept people, patting and other dogs because it *wants* to, not because it is forced to stay in position.

Introduce the exercises in a safe area free from traffic. Later on you can practise with your dog on the lead to simulate everyday situations such as walking your dog down the street and meeting other people and their dogs.

You will be most successful in teaching these lessons if you take them one step at a time. Always make the lessons fun for your dog and you should be able to progress rapidly. Teach in short sessions with your dog really eager for food. Here's how you can go about it:

Teaching the Lessons

Sitting politely while it's patted

1 Sit or stand your dog at your left-hand side, see Lessons 2 and 3.

2 Ask a friend to approach your dog from the front, but slightly towards the dog's left side, and walk past close to the dog. As your friend passes, give your dog a piece of food.

3 Repeat point 2 until your dog gets used to this procedure.

4 Next, ask your friend to approach your dog and stroke it briefly on the chest. Reinforce your dog as this happens. Repeat this a few times.

5 When your dog has become used to being patted on the chest ask your friend to touch various parts of its body, including patting it on the head and on its rump. Food induce good responses continuously at first and then reinforce intermittently *after* the dog has been touched.

Continue practising this exercise with lots of different people—men, women and children—using people that the dog knows first of all and then as many strangers as possible.

When your dog can be touched anywhere while it sits or stands at your left-hand side, you can progress to the next stage where your dog is touched when you are not close to it. This will simulate a common situation during walks when children run up to your dog to pat it, or when two people meet and pat one another's dogs.

6 Leave your dog in a Sit or Stand Stay, see Lesson 5, and stand *directly* in front of your dog.

7 Follow the procedure as before, i.e. ask a friend to touch your dog and feed it as this happens.

8 Repeat point 7 a few times.

9 Progress to a point where your dog can be touched all over its body and then reinforce *after* the touching has finished.

10 Gradually increase the distance between you and your dog until it will sit quietly and happily while it is being patted when you are not next to it. Then go back to your original position beside the dog and reinforce it intermittently.

Accepting a friendly stranger

Repeat points 4 and 5 on page 75, but ask your friend to shake hands with you instead of touching your dog. Reinforce your dog intermittently for remaining calm.

Reacting calmly to another dog

Once your dog is thoroughly conditioned to meeting people calmly on a lead, you can progress to meeting another person with a dog that has been trained to at least the same level.

1 Walk towards the other person and, when you come to within 2 metres (6 feet) of each other, sit your dogs.

2 Each handler should reinforce their own dog.

3 Gradually bring the dogs closer together, reinforcing them intermittently, until you are sure that your dog will remain calm even when it is very close to the other dog.

Meeting another person and patting each other's dogs

Before you attempt this, both dogs must be well conditioned to stay still for patting on their own. The procedure of patting your friend's dog and then returning to reinforce your own is exactly the same as previously shown.

B. Grooming

Ideally you should start grooming your dog when it is very young within a few days of bringing it home. However, it is never too late.

Condition your dog to accept patting first so that it welcomes being touched all over, see Exercise A.

Teaching *the Lessons*

1 Select a grooming implement which is suitable for your dog's coat type.

2 It is probably better to start with your dog lying down as it is more likely to be relaxed in this position. Squat down by its side and gently stroke its body with your left hand, then immediately reinforce it with food from your right hand.

3 Repeat point 2 but use a wide toothed comb or brush instead of your hand. At this stage it doesn't really matter if you are grooming your dog efficiently. You are simply conditioning it to like the process.

4 Gradually increase the amount of grooming you do before offering a reinforcement. Build this up gradually over a number of days so that your dog doesn't get sick of it. Be careful never to hurt your dog when you are grooming, i.e. comb out any tangles very gently, or you will have to go back to point 2 and build up its confidence again.

Maintain this conditioning in the usual manner.

You are now ready to teach your dog to be touched on a table as a precursor to the more elaborate veterinary examination.

Getting your dog used to being put on a table

First practise the next part *at home* with a friend.

5 Offer your dog a small piece of food and, while it is occupied with eating, pick it up and place it on a table. Then reinforce it again *on* the table. Very large heavy dogs can be conditioned to stand on a broad ramp. The idea is always to ensure that your dog enjoys the process.

6 Repeat point 5 a few times.

7 Progress until you can place your dog on the table, then intermittently reinforce it when it is quiet.

8 Now teach your dog to accept being touched on any part of its body by repeating the conditioning procedure you practised for points 3 and 4, i.e. touch a part gently, then reinforce. Practise opening the mouth and cleaning the teeth and ears. Be careful *never* to reinforce your dog if it backs off from a touch, otherwise you will reinforce fearful behaviour, instead of bold confident responses.

If your dog *does* back off, go back to the start of the conditioning procedure and progress *slowly* from there, remembering to keep the sessions short and enjoyable.

9 When your dog has learned to be examined all over its body when it's on the table, you must start to reinforce it intermittently to maintain good reliable responses.

Now you are ready to repeat the procedure with a friend or veterinarian conducting the 'examination'.

C. Veterinary Examination

It is unfortunate that a puppy's first experience in a veterinary clinic may well be an aversive one. Vets have to immunise pups and having an injection is not the most pleasant experience in the world. Responsible breeders take their litters to a vet for immunisation at about 6 weeks of age, 2 weeks before they go to their new homes. Medically this is obviously the correct procedure but it does mean that the new owner rarely has control over the pup's first veterinary experience and their pup may already associate the sights and smells of a clinic with something unpleasant.

Somehow we have to persuade dogs that going to the vet is not traumatic. The *ideal* situation is one where puppy socialisation classes take place in vets' clinics. Vets have told us that pups who attend these classes really love coming to the clinic in later life. It's a question of conditioning the dog when it is at its most receptive. There is only one possible disadvantage: the pups may be slightly more at risk of contracting disease in a vet's clinic than in a 'clean' outdoor area, in the same way that people are more likely to contract an infection in hospital! However, the risks of not socialising your dog are very much greater, see Chapter 2.

Teaching *the Lesson*

1 Try to get your vet's permission to enter the waiting room, sit your dog, reinforce it with a large piece of food, and then take it away from the clinic! Your dog must be super keen for food so that the reinforcement has great significance.

2 Repeat point 1 a number of times so that your dog just loves going there.

3 Ask your vet or the vet nurse to reinforce your dog in the clinic. These are just social visits, the vet does not examine your dog or treat it in any way.

4 The next stage is the proper vet examination. By this time your dog should be looking forward to visits to the vet. Place it on the examination table and reinforce it. Ask your vet to reinforce bold happy responses occasionally. It is well worth your vet's time and effort as a quiet, happy dog is much easier to handle than one which will not stay still. It may also save your dog from having to be anaesthetised for a minor procedure such as clipping hair round an area of eczema or having its ears examined.

Now, you may ask yourself, 'What do I do if my dog has an injection and it shows concern about this?' Simply, do not reinforce that response. Then try to produce a number of positive responses and reinforce at the end of these. Be aware that *reinforcement should not be offered too close to an undesirable response, otherwise the whole repertoire may be likely to be repeated in future.* After all, that is why we reinforce behaviour!

Lesson 7

Out for a Walk
(Including Doing a Turn)

Why should an Ideal Dog Walk Politely on a Loose Lead?

A pleasant walk with a dog can turn into a nightmare when it constantly pulls at the end of a lead. It can get so bad that the poor owner is virtually being towed along the street and the dog appears to be the one in control, rather than vice versa. This kind of dog is certainly not an ideal one! It would be difficult to take through a crowd of people, will probably barge through doorways and is certainly not safe for young children or elderly people to handle.

Pulling on the lead is often the result of what might be called the 'short lead syndrome'. Some people feel that their dog is under better control if it is forced to walk right next to them. Inadvertently they are teaching their dog to pull! The dog lunges forward to smell something interesting and the owner wrenches it back. The dog wheezes, chokes, comes back beside the owner for a moment, then surges ahead again. The whole scenario is repeated throughout the walk. However, the good news is that it's fairly easy to teach a dog to walk nicely on the lead, although it does require more co-ordination and timing on the part of the handler than more static lessons such as the Sit and the Stay.

Your ideal dog can be controlled under any circumstances

Teaching *the Lesson*

It is much better to teach a dog to heel *off lead* first, as some dogs can actually be triggered to pull as soon as a lead is clipped onto their collar. Begin by practising in a restricted environment if your dog has already developed a tendency to pull.

Make sure your dog will always come back to you before you let it off the lead in an open area.

1 Start with your dog in a sit or stand position at your left-hand side. Carry a few pieces of food in your left hand and one piece in your right. Keep your hands at waist level except when you are offering a signal.

2 Step off with your left leg, simultaneously sweeping your right hand forward parallel to your dog at its eye level. Say 'Heel' as you both move off together.

3 Move your right hand back to its original position at waist level as you take a few brisk paces.

4 After a few paces, signal your dog to stand, as shown in Lesson 3, and reinforce your dog instantly.

5 Take another piece of food in your right hand and repeat points 2 to 4 a number of times.

6 Gradually increase the distance you cover before you reinforce your dog. Eliminate the use of food as a stimulus and start to reinforce your dog intermittently.

7 Practise in short bursts in different environments so that your dog responds under different conditions and with a variety of distractions; it is fairly useless training your dog so that it only responds in your own backyard! Make sure you practise with other dogs around.

NOTE: Try not to fall into the habit of stopping if your dog does not come with you, otherwise it is really training you instead of the other way around! Keep moving until it feels stressed to come after you, then offer a more interesting signal next time! Timing and anticipation are critical during the heeling exercise.

Once your dog is well conditioned to walk beside you off the lead, it is then a simple matter to practise the same actions on lead. Offer exactly the same signals and you will get the same response!

It is preferable to use a long, light lead and heel with a distinct loop between you and the dog. The lead should only be used to keep your dog safe or to comply with local government rules and regulations. It should never be used violently to jerk the dog or hold it forcibly in position. The use of force is a clear indication that the dog has not been properly trained and the handler is inexperienced. If you see someone hauling their dog along, perhaps you may be able to help them to teach it more effectively.

Turning during Heeling

We cannot keep moving forwards in the same direction all the time so it is useful to be able to turn quickly without pulling on the lead. Below we show you how to do a right about turn, i.e. you and your dog turn 180 degrees to the right so that you walk back on the same line as you were travelling before the turn. The right and left turn are taught in Lesson 8.

Teaching *the Lesson*

1 Heel your dog at your left-hand side. Make sure that it is close to your left leg before you attempt the turn.

2 When you want to turn, drop your right hand containing food to a point slightly in front of your right leg, level with your dog's nose.

3 As your dog steps across to investigate your hand, pivot on the spot 180 degrees. Your dog will follow your moving hand as you turn provided you complete the turn fairly slowly on the first few occasions.

4 When you have completed the turn swing your right hand forward in the usual manner for heeling. Take a few paces then reinforce your dog with the food in your hand.

5 Repeat points 1 to 4 a few times, gradually increasing the speed of the turn. If you want, you can phase out the use of a hand signal as your dog gets used to your body movements.

6 Maintain conditioning as usual by eliminating food as an inducement and intermittently reinforcing really good tight turns.

Lesson 8

Walking Through a Crowd

Why should an Ideal Dog Walk Calmly Through a Crowd?

How will your dog behave if you are walking it on a crowded pavement and you see a blind person with a white cane ahead of you or a pregnant lady with a small child in tow? The last thing you want is for your dog's lead to get tangled around their legs; in fact no one wants to meet an unruly dog! Walking past people with your dog in a controlled manner and changing direction may sound like a simple procedure but it needs practice. Here's how you can teach your dog to do it effortlessly.

Teaching the Lessons

We suggest that you teach your dog to avoid stationary objects first, then progress to weaving through a group of moving people and then, even more difficult, through a number of people and their dogs. Arrange a few household objects such as rubbish bins or large flower pots to act as obstacles.

A. Turning towards your right

Practise on the lead so that you get used to handling it.

1 Heel your dog towards the first object.

2 As you come close to the object, drop your right hand containing food in front of your dog's nose.

3 Now swing this hand across your body at the dog's eye level and turn your own body towards the right. The dog will change direction with you. Make sure that it turns close to your left side so that the lead does not get tangled around the obstacle.

4 Then heel off in the normal manner.

B. Turning towards your left

1 As you approach the first obstacle drop your left hand containing food in front of your dog's face at its eye level.

2 Move your left hand out to your left so that your dog is induced to move out from your body. If you don't induce your dog to move away from you, you may knock into it with your left leg as you turn.

3 As your dog moves left, you must move with it so that there is no danger of tangling the lead around the obstacle.

4 Then heel off in the normal manner.

NOTE: You can use your left hand to offer the heel signal if you wish, so that you do not have to use two different hands for offering signals.

5 Once you have practised turning towards your right and left through obstacles, you can then do the same past one or two people. You may have to offer a more demonstrative signal so that your dog is stimulated to come with *you* rather than going over to say 'Hello' to the people in the 'crowd'.

6 Gradually increase the number of people in your 'crowd' and ask them to move around, talk and even jostle one another so that your dog learns to cope with all kinds of situations.

C. Right and left turns

If the test in your country requires that you do right and left turns when you are heeling on lead, this means that you have to change direction at a 90 degree angle. The technique is the same as for A and B, see the photographs on pages 85 and 86.

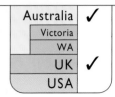

Australia	✓
Victoria	
WA	
UK	✓
USA	

Lesson 9

Walking Through a Door or Gate

Why should an Ideal Dog Go Through a Doorway under Control?

We go in and out of doors dozens of times a day and how many times have we nearly been tripped up by a dog barging through in front of us? How much better it would be if we could teach our dogs that *we* should go through first!

Here's how to do it. Like many of the lessons required for the assessments you will be combining a number of exercises which you have already learnt, i.e. the Sit or Stand, the Wait and Heel on lead. (Lessons 2, 3, 5 and 7)

Teaching *the Lesson*

1 Put your dog on a light lead and heel it up to a gate or doorway.

2 Sit or stand your dog and then say 'Wait'. Open the door or gate.

3 Allow the lead to hang loose and step through the doorway yourself.

4 Call your dog to you through the doorway, taking up any excess slackness in the lead.

Option 1

5 Heel off and reinforce your dog after you have walked a few paces.

Option 2

5 If you want to close the door or gate, do a right-about-turn after your dog has joined you and sit your dog so that you are both facing the door again. Say 'Wait', then step forward and close the door. Do another right-about-turn and heel off with your dog. Reinforce your dog after you have walked a few paces.

6 Practise in different environments with different types of openings. Make sure that you go through doors first at home so that your dog does not get mixed messages.

Lesson 10

Remaining Calm when Distractions are Present

Why should an Ideal Dog Cope with Distractions?

It is important that dogs are not upset by all the numerous sights and sounds of urban living. This is why it is necessary to socialise your dog to different animals and habituate it to all sorts of sounds from a very early age (Chapter 2).

The Australian and USA assessments specify that dogs shouldn't show fear when they are exposed to various everyday situations although they may show a startle response, i.e be surprised. The requirements vary slightly, see the assessment programmes in the Appendix; however, your dog should be able to cope with all of them and many more if it is to live happily in a built-up area.

We will describe the teaching procedure in two sections. The first four situations deal with controlling your dog when there is activity around and it may be stimulated to chase or jump up.

Activities

A   A jogger running near the dog
B   A person pushing a shopping trolley within 3 metres (9 feet) of the dog
C   A person riding a bicycle within 2 metres (6 feet) of the dog
D   A person using crutches, a stick, a walking frame or a wheelchair
E   Other handlers and dogs walking past

We'll use the cyclist as an example because it is the situation which is most likely to produce a hunt and chase response, but the same principles apply to the other five situations listed above.

Teaching the Lesson

Put your dog on a long lead so that, if the worst comes to the worst, you can prevent it from actually chasing the moving object. Established bicycle chasers will take longer to condition.

Place your dog in a sit position at your left-hand side, see Lesson 2.

2 Ask a friend to cycle *slowly* past in *front* of you at about a 5 to 10 metres (15 to 30 feet) distance. Food induce your dog while it sits and stays as the bicycle goes by. It is important that you feed the dog at exactly the same moment as the bicycle passes so that it *prefers* to stay with you.

3 Repeat point 2 a number of times gradually increasing the speed of the bicycle.

4 Progress to a point where the bicycle passes you and *then* reinforce your dog. Reinforce it each time on about 6 occasions, then intermittently as usual.

5 Gradually bring the bicycle closer to the dog until you have conditioned it to stay still as the bicycle passes within 2 metres (6 feet) or even closer.

Practise with the bicycle coming from all sorts of positions including from behind the dog which is a common situation when you are out walking in the park.

Noises

The second section involves teaching your dog to get used to various sounds which could be threatening to a naive dog.

A   *A chair falling over about 2 metres (6 feet) away from the dog.*
B   *The sudden opening or closing of a door.*
C   *Dropping a large book at least 3 metres (9 feet) behind the dog.*

D   *People jostling one another and appearing excited within 3 metres (9 feet) of the dog, see also Lesson 8.*

We suggest that you follow a procedure similar to the one we have already described. Again we will choose one situation as our example, i.e dropping a book behind the dog.

Teaching *the Lesson*

1 Sit your dog at your left-hand side.

2 Ask a friend to drop a light object such as a paperback about 3 metres (9 feet) in *front* of your dog so that the dog can see what's happening. You don't want to startle the dog if you can help it. As your friend drops the book, feed your dog. Good timing is critical as you must pair the benefit of the food with the presence of the noise.

3 Practise point 2 a few times. If your dog's reaction is fine and it shows no fear, you can gradually build up the size and the weight of the dropped object.

4 Follow the same routine when you drop the book at the side of your dog, and then behind it.

5 Progress to a point where your friend can drop the article then reinforce your dog *after* good responses.

6 It is a good idea to treat each new position as a 'new' exercise. That is, reinforce good responses continuously in each position about 6 times and then start reinforcing intermittently.

7 If your dog shows even the slightest fear or anxiety, do *not* reinforce that behaviour. Go back to point 1 and build up your conditioning more slowly next time.

Follow the same procedure with shutting and slamming doors and any other noise your dog is likely to be exposed to such as the lawn mower and the vacuum cleaner.

Most dogs will learn to cope very quickly, but don't take it for granted. We know of dogs that are so anxious when they hear thunder or a balloon burst that it is really difficult for their handlers to re-condition them. This can happen because of inadequate socialisation at a critical age or through 'superstitious learning', that is learning by association. An example of superstitious learning occurs when a small child is given an injection by a doctor wearing a white coat. Anyone wearing a white coat may cause anxiety to the child in the future.

In situations such as this you will have to desensitise your dog very gradually to the fearful situation, using the process we have already explained, but you will need to progress much more slowly.

It is better to practise a few different exercises when you train your dog rather than concentrate on one. For example, you could 'revise' some previous lessons or teach an active one which your dog really enjoys after you've practised a more passive one. Most dogs get bored with too much repetition and some appear to get worried if you repeat an exercise too often. It's almost as if they are saying 'What have I done wrong?!' So work on a few different lessons for a short time and have fun.

Getting Used to Being Left Without the Handler

Why should an Ideal Dog Become Used to Being Left Alone for a Short Time?

Books on Roman history often illustrate large dogs chained to a wall, standing sentinel in front of their master's villa. Their posture and facial expression suggest that they were in defensive mode, very like many of today's dogs when they are left tied to a post while their owner goes into a shop! (This is not an activity we recommend, but in real life it often happens.)

Like human beings, dogs were not born to have chains around their necks, nor do they willingly endure restraint. People often unwittingly teach tethered dogs to lunge at them by half-heartedly presenting their hands to the dog, then quickly withdrawing them thinking that it might bite. The dog's initial friendly approach can easily develop into a feeling of insecurity. It cannot run away because of the lead so it

is likely to become conditioned to snap. Animals under stress choose *fight* or *flight* and if we prevent the latter they have no choice but to fight. Leads must be the bane of dogs' lives!

However, if the same dog is on a 5-metre (15 foot) lead its reactions will be almost identical to that of a totally free dog. So when you start conditioning your dog to enjoy being tied up, tie it up on a long lead.

The assessments involve either leaving the dog alone for a short time tied up on a lead or leaving it with a stranger holding it. The dog should be able to wait reasonably calmly and should not lunge or bark continuously. Getting a dog to Stay when the owner is not in sight can, and often does, offer some problems, see Lesson 5. So, let's make the path to success as smooth as possible.

Getting Ready

You will need:
   (a) a 3 to 4 metre (9 to 12 feet) long lead,
   (b) somewhere to hide,
   (c) food reinforcements, and
   (d) the assistance of a friend.
NOTE: You don't have to leave your dog in any spe-

cific position for this exercise so choose the one you want. The Sit is probably the easiest for the dog. The dog is *not* required to remain in a Stay position although this lesson will be much easier to teach if you have already practised Lesson 5 because your dog will be used to being left for a short time.

Teaching *the Lesson*

We assume that you have already taught your dog the Stay and that you can produce a dependable 'Stay' response when you step a few paces away from your dog.

You can hide behind such things as a building or a tree. We have used a tree for our example as it was easier to photograph!

1 Place yourself and your dog a few paces away from a tree. Your dog should be on a long loose lead which is attached to a pole or stake, or a friend can hold your dog depending on the requirements in your country.

2 Say 'Wait' to your dog and offer the usual Stay hand signal, then take 3 or 4 steps forward towards the tree.

3 Go back and reinforce your dog for remaining quiet on the end of the lead.

4 Repeat points 2 and 3 a number of times, then progressively go further away from your dog reinforcing it intermittently on your return.

5 This time, step off to the tree, about turn, and then step briefly behind the tree. Step back in sight of the dog, pause for a second, then return to your dog. Reinforce immediately.

6 Repeat this procedure several times, gradually increasing the time out of sight. Ask your friend to observe your dog's response when you are away from it.

7 Increase the distance between the out of sight position and your dog, and the time that you leave your dog alone or with another person, until you can fulfil the criteria for assessment in your country. You can also gradually shorten the length of the lead until you fulfill the necessary requirements.

8 Finally, get a few friends to stroll around your dog while the exercise is in progress. They can touch the dog briefly and examine its tags to simulate an official checking the registration.

Lesson 12

Calming Your Dog After Play
(Giving up an Article)

Why should an Ideal Dog Give up an Article or Toy?

Most dogs love chasing sticks or toys. If they could throw things they would amuse themselves for hours! Chasing articles which are hurtling through the air allows dogs to mimic the hunting, grabbing, chasing behaviour seen in wolves when pursuing prey. Having caught a large animal wolves generally dine together leaving just a bloodstain in the snow. However, when an individual wolf breaks off a piece of the carcass it will take its prize to a quiet spot and possess it, so to speak. 'It's mine,' says the wolf. 'I'm not giving it up.' Some dogs have the same attitude!

It seems a bit presumptuous to try to interfere with millions of years of natural development and ask our dogs to give up their sticks and toys. Once they're in the mouth of some dogs you can almost hear them say 'possession is nine-tenths the law!'

NOT SO FAST MR WOLF!

If we humans can create computers surely we can develop a way of inducing a dog to give up its toy willingly. This is especially important with some breeds such as Cocker Spaniels who are notoriously possessive. Dogs who have not learnt to give things up may growl, and even bite, in an attempt to retain a favoured object, particularly if a child approaches them.

Many dogs, especially when they are young, get so excited that they find it very difficult to stop playing a game, any game. This exercise will help you to teach your dog to calm down after play or patting. Look back at Lessons 5 and 10 before you teach this one. It is important because many accidents with dogs, especially ones with children, occur when a dog gets overexcited during play. On the other hand, some dogs are so placid that their owners will be wondering what all the fuss is about!

'How do we teach the exercise?' you may say. 'Easily if you follow these actions.'

'This one's mine!'

Teaching the Lesson

NOTE: If your dog is not interested in holding things in its mouth, there is no need to teach this lesson.

Prepare your dog so that it is keen for food and place some chopped up pieces of food in a bag in your pocket, or around your waist.

1 Offer your dog an article, which you know it likes, with one hand.

2 As it grabs at the article, immediately offer it a piece of food from your other hand. *Do not release the article* otherwise the dog may run away with it.

3 As the dog releases the article to take the food say 'Give'.

4 Repeat points 1 to 3 several times.

5 Now that your dog has learnt the word 'Give' you can actually give it the article. Allow the dog to hold it for a few seconds, then say 'Give' and take it from the dog.

6 Repeat point 5 a few times but offer food *intermittently.*

Combining Retrieving with Giving up an Article

This is not a requirement of any of the assessments but it is a fun exercise for you and your dog and provides the dog with lots of exercise.

Teaching the Lesson

1 Take a piece of food in your left hand. Throw an article a few paces away from your dog with your right hand, making sure that it tumbles along the ground so that your dog is stimulated to chase after it.

2 The moment your dog chases after the article say 'Fetch' and simultaneously move forward after your dog so that, when it picks up the article, you are not too far away from it.

3 As soon as the dog reaches the article and picks it up in its mouth, move rapidly away from your dog with your back towards it so it wants to chase after you.

4 When your dog has caught up with you, and not before, spin around quickly offering food to the dog with your left hand as you take the article with your right. Say 'Give'. The exchange of food for the article will look good to the dog. In fact, both the dog and the handler are thinking the same thing. 'What you've got is what I want!'

NOTE: Handlers who have had difficulty in getting their dogs to come when called will quickly realise that the retrieving exercise can be a great teaching aid. Your dog goes away from you and is then triggered to return to you for more fun. This is just another example of the dog finding it beneficial to respond as *you* want!

Lesson 13

Road Safety
(Getting Out of a Car Under Control)

Why should an Ideal Dog Get Out of a Car Under Control?

Sometimes getting a dog out of a car can look like a Charlie Chaplin movie! The moment the door is opened the dog barges past the owner like a rugby forward or a grid iron player! The owner, knocked off balance by the swinging door and desperately holding onto the lead, finishes up spread eagled over the contours of the car. Parcels are abandoned. All hope is lost! Now let's rewind the tape and start again.

The lesson combines two exercises: teaching your dog to wait in any position while a car door is opened and jumping down when given a signal to do so. It is a very important lesson for you and your dog and may even save your dog's life. Suppose, for example,

that you have a puncture on a busy highway and your dog is sitting in the back of the car on top of the spare tyre!

We are going to use the Sit position for our example, but you can choose either the Sit, Stand or Drop. You have already taught your dog the Sit and Stay in Lessons 2 and 5. Make sure that you can do them successfully before you teach this lesson.

We use a station wagon or hatchback to teach this exercise as it is more difficult to get a dog to Stay in these types of cars. If you can teach your dog satisfactorily with this type of vehicle, then you will easily be able to repeat the lesson in a smaller sedan.

Teaching the Lesson

1 Use a stationary car which is parked off the road in an area safe from traffic.

2 Induce the dog to jump into the back of the car or lift it in. Do not shut the door. If it is not your car let the dog sniff around a bit until it gets used to any strange smells. Some dogs can become quite excited if they smell an unfamiliar odour, especially of another animal.

3 Take a piece of food in one hand. Say 'Sit'. Once your dog has adopted the correct position, say 'Wait' and, at the same time, make the usual Stay hand signal with the other hand, see Lesson 5.

4 Leaving the car door open, step away from the car for a couple of paces, then return to your original position and reinforce the dog.

5 Practise points 3 and 4 a few times, going further from the vehicle each time and start to reinforce your dog intermittently. This will teach your dog that it is beneficial to wait quietly in the car when signalled to do so.

6 Next say 'Wait' and pull the back door of the car down a short distance with one arm. Lift it back up and reinforce your dog.

7 Gradually progress until you can pull the car door right down, and your dog will remain quiet and wait while you close it and then reopen it. It doesn't matter if your dog changes position.

8 Repeat point 7 but this time clip on the dog's lead, then reinforce the dog for remaining still in the car.

9 Now you are ready to practise in a more realistic setting. Drive the car to any safe destination—perhaps a quiet car park. Stop the car and go around to the back door as you normally do. Say 'Sit' and 'Wait' as usual, open the door and clip on the lead. Your dog should be thoroughly conditioned to do this by now but remember that different environments sometimes trigger different responses.

10 Keep the lead loose in one hand and get a piece of food ready in the other. Don't wave it in the dog's face.

11 Offer a visual signal by pointing to the ground with one hand to encourage your dog to jump down. Say 'Down' at the same time so that you pair the word with the dog's response.

12 When it has jumped down, signal your dog to sit and wait, then reinforce it.

13 Close the car door and immediately give your dog another piece of food for remaining calm and quiet beside you.

14 Heel off in the usual way. If possible reward your dog with a good run.

15 Practise the whole exercise in lots of different settings, including situations where other dogs are gathered outside the car. If you can do the exercise under these conditions, you should be able to do it anywhere! Remember punctures don't often happen in ideal locations.

NOTE: The word 'Down' is used for this exercise whereas the word 'Drop' is used when you want your dog to lie down.

The word 'Wait' is used instead of 'Stay' as you are going to ask the dog to move out of the Stay position.

Lesson 14

Meal Time Manners

Why should an Ideal Dog Learn Good Meal Time Manners?

Once it was quite normal for a family to sit down at the dinner table and wait for the father's permission to eat. Table manners were strictly enforced. A dog's meal time etiquette is quite different. To them a piece of food in the mouth is worth a chunk in the hand and to say to a wolf 'Steady on old fella you can only eat when I say so' is trying to change its very nature.

However, to help the wolf in our home live in our society we have to develop behaviours which give it a sporting chance of survival. Our dogs are expected not to jump up and knock us over to get at their food. The ideal time to start this training is when the dog is very young, preferably between 8 and 12 weeks old. But, whatever the age, the method of teaching is the same.

Teaching *the Lesson*

You will need an empty food bowl.

1 Sit your dog at your left-hand side. Take a small piece of *delicious* food such as meat in your *left* hand.

2 Feed your dog with the delicious morsel from your *left* hand as you place the empty bowl on the floor in front of it with your *right*. Say 'Stay, Leave it', then quickly pick up the bowl before your dog shows too much interest in it.

3 Repeat point 2 a few times until your dog shows no interest in the bowl.

4 Next put the bowl down on the floor as you say 'Stay, Leave it' and *then* reinforce your dog's response *after* it has left the bowl alone.

5 Repeat points 2 to 4 a few times, first with uninteresting (to your dog) food in the dish such as diced carrots and then more appealing things such as dry dog food.

Some people get worried that their dog will try to grab the food so they give their signals in a rather threatening manner. Avoid this or your dog will get anxious about the lesson.

6 Finally progress to a point where you can place a bowl on the ground which contains the dog's usual meal and say 'Stay, Leave it'.

7 Pause for a few seconds before pointing to the food bowl and saying 'Yours', or whatever word you wish.

8 Gradually increase the time between putting the bowl down and saying 'Yours'. Vary the time factor daily so that the dog cannot predict how long it will have to wait.

If you do this exercise every day at meal times, your dog will be like Rin Tin Tin within a week!

NOTE: If you wish, you can drop the word 'Stay' when your dog becomes conditioned to the words 'Leave it'.

Promoting Responsible Dog Ownership

The message in this book is that education is the key to happiness and safety for ourselves and for our dogs. One way of ensuring that prospective dog owners learn about their responsibilities to their pets and to the general public is to require them to obtain a permit *before* they can get a dog, just as we have to get a Driver's Licence before we can drive a car. This would virtually eliminate impulse buying of pets in such places as markets and would give local authorities an opportunity to check that a resident has adequate facilities to house a dog. It would be best if a permit be granted only after the prospective owner had undertaken a short course, free of charge, on the responsibilities of pet ownership. In this way they would be given the opportunity of deciding whether dog ownership is a responsibility they want to assume before they take the irrevocable step of getting a dog. If this simple but revolutionary idea were implemented many of our current dog problems would disappear within a few years.

In order to stop people getting a dog without authority, a numbered permit would have to be produced before the dog could be registered. A table of reduced registration fees for pensioners and working or service dogs would ensure that the system did not prevent caring people from having a dog because they could not afford it. Penalties for owning unregistered dogs could be much higher! Dog owners who train their dogs to be Ideal Dogs or Good Citizens could be rewarded by paying a much lower registration fee than normal, as another incentive to encourage responsible dog ownership. The system of lower registration fees for trained dogs has already been introduced in some states in Australia and the USA so perhaps our proposal is not all that utopian!

If most of the money raised from registration fees were allocated to educating dog owners about their responsibilities and schoolchildren about animal welfare, then it wouldn't be necessary to put a lot of money into the maintenance of such things as pounds and the prevention of cruelty to animals.

Local councils are in an ideal position to supervise this kind of scheme and there is little doubt that, in the long run, it would save them much time and trouble. However, such a radical change in public perception to the belief that dog ownership is a privilege not a right would require the kind of promotional scheme that only governments and multinationals seem able to fund. Meanwhile the expansion of such programmes as the Ideal Dogs of Australia scheme and Canine Good Citizen and the efforts of individuals and organisations to educate the public in responsible behaviour towards dogs may perhaps pave the way for more far-reaching reforms designed to make our cities and suburbs safe for dogs.

Glossary

The Technical Term	An Example
Unconditioned stimulus	Food
Conditioned stimuli	Voice and hand signals
Unconditioned response	A response to food in the hand
Conditioned response	A response to the voice and hand signal
Positive reinforcement	Anything beneficial to the dog
Primary or unconditioned reinforcement	Food
Secondary or conditioned reinforcement	Pat. 'Good boy.'
Punishment	An aversive event, e.g a jerk in the neck with a choke chain. (Not used in our method.)
Negative reinforcement	The cessation of punishment, e.g. the choke chain going slack. (Not used in our method.)

Ideal Dogs of Australia Assessment

The Ideal Dogs of Australia Assessment

DOGS UNDERTAKING THIS TEST MUST SHOW NO FEAR OR AGGRESSION TOWARD HUMANS. ANY OWNER WHO USES ANY TYPE OF PHYSICAL OR VERBAL FORCE OR COMPULSION WILL NOT BE PERMITTED TO CONTINUE THE ASSESSMENT.

Lessons learnt in the Ideal Dogs of Australia Course should simulate everyday life as much as possible. The course is designed to give dog owners a good understanding about how they can train their dogs to be well behaved pets. The emphasis is on enjoyment and participation. At the completion of the course, participants should have a sound knowledge about dog behaviour and training.

All exercises must be completed off lead unless otherwise stated. No food inducement is allowed. Reinforcement may be offered at the completion of each exercise if appropriate.

All 10 assessments must be completed satisfactorily.

A certificate and dog tag will be awarded to handlers and dogs which successfully pass the Ideal Dogs of Australia Assessment.

1 Controlled Walk

The dog should walk in a controlled manner beside the handler without pulling on a lead for 50 paces including making a turn and doing a sit and drop.

The lead must be between 2 and 3 metres (6 and 9 feet) long. (Formal heeling at the handler's left-hand side is not required.) During the walk the dog will go through a door or gateway under control. (Lessons 2, 4, 7 and 9.)

2 Walking through a Crowd

The dog should walk through a group of at least 5 people in a controlled manner. The distance will be a minimum of 20 paces and the dog must be on a loose lead. (Lessons 7 and 8.)

3 Reaction to Distractions

The dog should remain under control when distractions are present such as a bicycle, pram or jogger passing by. The distraction is to pass within 5 paces of the dog. The dog should then be offered an article and demonstrate that it will give it up readily. (Lessons 2, 5, 10 and 12.)

4 Veterinary Examination

The dog should be able to be patted and handled by someone who is not the owner, including being touched on the head and in the mouth. The dog may be in any position of the handler's choice and need not remain in a stay position. The dog must not jump up or show any avoidance behaviour. (Lessons 2 and 6.)

5 Reaction to another Dog

The dog should greet another dog which has proven to be temperamentally sound without showing fear or aggression. Both dogs must be on lead. (Lessons 2, 5 and 6.)

6 The Recall

The dog should come when called off lead from a distance of 20 paces. It need not be left in a stay position but can be held by the tester if required until the handler is 20 paces away. (Lesson 1.)

7 Stay in Positon

The dog should stay in the drop, sit or stand position for a period of 15 seconds with the handler at a distance of 5 paces. (Lessons 2, 3, 4, and 5.)

8 Supervised Tolerance to Separation

The dog should be left tied up with the handler out of sight for a period of 30 seconds. The dog need not stay in one position, but should remain calm.
A number of people should be able to pass close to the dog without it lunging at them. (Lessons 5 and 11.)

9 Road Safety

The dog should remain calm while a car door is opened and a lead is attached to its collar. It should then leave the car and remain on a loose lead while the handler closes the car door. (Lessons 2, 5 and 13.)

10 Meal Time Manners

The dog must sit and wait while a small bowl of food is placed on the ground in front of it. It must remain in the sit position until the signal to eat is given. The dog should allow the handler to remove the empty bowl without showing any resentment. (Lessons 2 and 14.)

Approved Dog Obedience Assessment Program

DOMESTIC (FERAL AND NUISANCE) ANIMALS
REGULATIONS 1996
ASSESSMENT CRITERIA

There are four areas where the handler and dog must achieve a pass to score an overall pass.

1 Heeling or walking the dog
2 Sociability test
3 Stay test
4 Recall test

* Consideration must be given to each dog's temperament, that is, character and physical being, when making the assessment.
* Where the overall test is failed, the handler may present the dog for a further test at a later date.
* The dog will automatically fail and not be awarded the certificate if during the assessment it displays aggression to other dogs or humans.

1 Walking the Dog

Dog to walk at heel or at least on a loose lead. This exercise must incorporate a minimum of three sit exercises. Handler must display reasonable control of the dog when walked, that is dog not to be pulling on a tight leash or jumping up on the handler, but be happy to follow the handler's commands or change of direction. (Lessons 2, 3, 7 and 8.)

In this test the handler may talk, handle and encourage the dog where necessary.

The dog will automatically fail this test if it displays any of the following behaviour traits:

* Bites the leash, i.e. in defiance such as tug-of-war, mouthing, etc.
* Walks in front of the handler continuously causing the handler to make allowances for the dog's unruly behaviour.
* Does not sit on command even after being corrected or guided.

2 Sociability Test

This is a two-part assessment where the dog is required to display no aggression towards dogs or people. It is to be conducted on a relaxed lead and under reasonable control.

(i) Human Sociability Test
The handler is to approach the assessor to within stroking distance. The dog should be under control and on a relaxed lead. If the dog displays any form of aggression towards the assessor or any other person it will be classified as a fail. Alternatively the assessor may approach the handler and dog. The dog must remain on a loose lead and under control. If it displays any aggression it will be failed. If it shies away but displays no aggression it will not be classified as a fail. (Lessons 6 and 7.)

(ii) Dog Sociability Test
The dog must be placed in a 'Sit at Heel' position beside the handler while other handlers and their dogs walk past on a lead. If the dog being tested shows aggression, it will be classified as a fail. (Lesson 2, 5 and 10.)

3 Stay Test

In this test the dog must remain in a Sit Stay position for one minute. The minimum distance the dog must be away from the handler is 2 metres. The leash may be attached. (Lessons 2 and 5.)

The dog is allowed minor movement, i.e. fidgeting or lying down in the Stay position. However, it must not run away. If the dog clearly breaks and takes flight, it is a fail.

The handler may talk to the dog and use encouragement where necessary.

4 The Recall Test

In this test the dog is to return to the handler on command from the required distance. The handler may use hand signals, multiple commands, whistle and any encouragement necessary to secure the return of the dog. The leash may be removed for this test.

There are two methods of assessment at the option of the handler.

Option 1
- Minimum distance away from the handler is 5 metres.
- The assessor may restrain the dog whilst the handler leaves to the required distance.
- Upon the assessor's signal the dog is to be called by the handler.
- More than one command may be used.
- It is not required that the dog sits when it approaches the handler.
- The dog must return to within the handler's reach so the handler may then secure the dog. (Lesson 1)

Option 2
- The handler is to release the dog from the lead and allow the dog to exercise freely while the handler walks casually. At the assessor's command and when the dog is at least 5 metres away from the handler, the handler is to call the dog. More than one command may be used and the dog is to return to the handler as in the recall test, Option 1. (Lesson 1)

NOTE: This approved course enables Victorian dog owners to qualify for lower licence registration fees. Phone Agriculture Victoria for details.

Canine Good Companion Programme

Copyright © The Canine Association of Western Australia Inc. Reprinted with kind permission from The Canine Association of Western Australia Inc., PO Box 301, Gosnells, WA 6110, telephone (09) 455 1188

CANINE GOOD COMPANION

DATE: ....DOG NO: ....BREED...
CLUB: ....NAME:..
EVALUATOR ....HANDLER:..

	TEST NO	DESCRIPTON	PASS	FAIL
1	APPEARANCE & GROOMING	Demonstrates the dog's willingness to be handled, groomed and examined by a stranger		
2	ACCEPT A STRANGER	Evaluator approaches, greets H in a friendly manner, ignoring dog. Dog must not strain or jump up.		
3	WALK ON LOOSE LEAD	Demonstrates that the dog is under control, but not "heeling" as required by the ANKC		
4	WALK THROUGH A CROWD	Under control whilst accompanying his handler through a group of at least 3, no pulling.		
5	SIT FOR EXAMINATION	Temperament and willingness to be talked to and patted by strangers.		
6	SIT AND DOWN	Demonstrates that the dog has had some formal training and is responsive, on move or stationary. Encourage, but no physical handling.		
7	SIT OR DOWN STAY 5m, 1/2 min	Demonstrates the dog's ability to remain calmly in position. Extra commands to position perm. Stay, drop lead, leave, 30 secs and return.		
8	REACTION	Proper behaviour when out walking and meeting another dog. 2 H approach from 10m, stop, comm. sit, shake hands and talk. Dogs to stay calm.		
9	DISTRACTION & RECALL	Demonstrates that the dog is confident, without showing fear or aggression and heeds H's call. THE EVALUATOR WILL SELECT TWO TESTS: a) A person on crutches, in a wheelchair or using a walker approaching the handler and dog from about 10m, passing by. b) The sudden opening or closing of a door. c) The sudden opening of umbrella at 2m from dog. d) Good natured pushing and shoving, passing within 3 metres. e) Shopping trolley approaching from front or rear. f) A jogger running front of the dog. g) A cyclist approaching from the front or rear, passing about 2m to the side of the dog. h) Handler and dog walking past grid in road, or over strange surface, metal grid, plastic sheeting or planks. Dog may express natural curiosity, may startle, must recover, should not panic, try to run away, be aggressive or bark. He should show confidence to approach feared object, relax, not pull away. Recall: Handler drops the lead as his dog is walking, when 5-10m away, handler may run away and clap hands.		
10	DOG LEFT SHOP STOP	Demonstrates dog's ability to wait patiently until his owner returns. The dog is not penalised for breaking from position provided he shows socially good manners. The dog is tied up, left in a down, handler out of sight close by for 3 minutes. The dog should not register anything stronger that mild agitation.		

lessons 2, 3, 4 and 6

lessons 2 and 5

lessons 3, 7 and 8

lessons 7 and 8

lessons 2, 5 and 6

lessons 2 and 4

lessons 2, 4 and 5

lessons 2, 5 and 6

lessons 2, 5 and 10

lesson 1

lessons 4, 5 and 11

PASS OR FAIL   JUDGE   SECRETARY
[CGCTEST.DOC]

THE KENNEL CLUB

Good Citizen Dog Scheme

Does your dog pass the test?

As part of the Good Citizen Scheme you will receive help in training your dog to be well behaved and will be given advice on grooming, exercise, diet and general health care. The Scheme is open to all dogs young and old, pedigree or crossbreeds. At the end of each course a Certificate is awarded to those passing a short Test.

For details of training courses please contact the Kennel Club on: 071 493 6651

THE KENNEL CLUB

Good Citizen Dog Scheme

You and your dog will be able to attend training sessions organised by a Kennel Club registered Club or other accredited organisation, details available from the Kennel Club (071 493 6651).

The Scheme is aimed at all dogs whether Kennel Club registered or not which have completed their vaccination programmes; there is no upper age limit.

The Test is straightforward and you will be taught to achieve the following:

1. Each handler must carry with them some form of "poop scoop" and all dogs must wear a collar and identification tag detailing the owner's name and address.

2. Put on collar and lead.

3. Walk on lead without distraction.

4. Walk on lead through Door/Gate.

5. Walk on lead passing people and dogs. Behave in controlled manner whilst owner holds a conversation for one minute.

6. Lie down and stay on command, on lead.

7. Groom.

8. Present for examination, on lead, including mouth, teeth, throat, eyes, ears and feet.

9. Release from lead, play with or without toy, recall and attach lead.

lesson 7

lessons 7 and 9

lessons 2, 3, 4, 7 and 8

lessons 4 and 5

lessons 2 and 6

lessons 2 and 6

lessons 1 and 12

Achieving a good partnership with your dog will prove to be one of the most rewarding relationships you will ever enter into; so become part of the *Kennel Club Good Citizen Dog Scheme.*

© The Kennel Club 1/94

THE KENNEL CLUB

1-5 Clarges Street, Piccadilly, London W1Y 8AB

THE KENNEL CLUB GOOD CITIZEN DOG SCHEME

Description

The Kennel Club Good Citizen Dog Scheme aims to produce a dog that will walk and sit in a controlled manner on the lead, will lie down on command, will allow its owner to clean and groom it and inspect its feet. The dog must also be able to be positioned by its owner for examination ie: stand, sit, lie down on either side or on its back, all on a lead. Lastly the dog must come to hand when called.

The Scheme is not competitive. Progress tests will be held at regular intervals, and a Certificate will be awarded when the required standard has been achieved.

The Scheme is aimed at all dogs whether Kennel Club registered or not which have completed their vaccination programmes; there is no upper age limit.

The final test is to be carried out under arrangement by the organising club by one of the following:-

(a) Dog Warden
(b) Recognised Kennel Club Judge
(c) Representative from the Institute of Professional Dog Trainers
(d) Police or Service Dog Handler

Test

1. Each handler must carry with them some form of "poop scoop" and all dogs must wear a collar and identification tag detailing the owner's name and address.

2. Put on collar and lead.

3. Walk on lead without distractions.

4. Walk on lead through Door/Gate.

5. Walk on lead passing people and dogs. Behave in controlled manner whilst owner holds a conversation for one minute.

6. Lie down and stay on command, on lead.

7. Groom.

8. Present for examination, on lead, including mouth, teeth, throat, eyes, ears and feet.

9. Release from lead, play with or without toy, recall and attach lead

lesson 7

lessons 7 and 9

lessons 2, 3, 4, 7 and 8

lessons 4 and 5

lessons 2 and 6

lessons 2 and 6

lessons 1 and 12

The examiner will enter the comment "Not Ready" or "Passed" alongside each exercise. The dogs must receive the comment "Passed" for each Exercise at one session in order to receive a Certificate.

Telephone: General Enquiries - 071-493 6651/629 5828 Registration Enquiries - 071-493 2001 Insurance - 0372 743472 Library - 071-499 0844

Explanation of Exercises

At the start of each training course each owner should be given a copy of the Canine Code; there should be a discussion period during which the importance of correct socialisation can be explained, problems discussed and advice given on choosing a suitable collar with identity disc and lead. The owner should be reminded that they must always remove any fouling caused by their dog and carry with them some form of "poop scoop".

1. Each handler must carry with them some form of "poop scoop" and all dogs must wear a collar and identification tag detailing the owner's name and address.

2. It is important that the collar and lead are suitable for type of dog and that the owner is able to fit them correctly.

3, 4, 5. The owner will be holding the lead with the dog by their side throughout these sections. The dog should walk on the left side of the handler without undue pulling forward or back (competition heelwork is not the aim). The dog must be able to stand, sit or lie down in a quiet relaxed manner whilst the owner is holding a conversation for 1 minute. This is not a stay exercise.

6. The exercise will be tested on lead. The dog to be placed in the down position with the lead attached to the collar. The lead be placed on the ground next to the dog and the owner will move a distance of 5 metres away for a period of 1 minute.

7. Grooming should be performed relevant to the individual dog.

8. The dog will be handled by the owner. This is a most important exercise and will require considerable care, expertise and patience on the part of the trainer. The dog will be required to be placed for examination of mouth, teeth, throat, eyes, ears and feet when standing, sitting and lying down (on either side or on its back). The average new owner may find these exercises difficult and frustrating. However, by involving the members of the class in examining each others' dogs under careful supervision success will be achieved.

9. The aim is to enable the owner to call the dog to him when released within a restricted area, ie., home or garden. There will be no requirement for the dog to sit, the owner will simply attach the lead to the collar which will not have been removed. The owner is to be advised not to let the dog run uncontrolled in open spaces such as woods, parks and farmland.

The Test is very basic and in order that it be meaningful the testing must be carried out rigorously. Any mouthing, growling or threatening behaviour is not acceptable and further training will be required before the dog can be passed.

Emphasis must be placed upon the ability of the owner to handle, care for and generally be responsible for their dog.

2/94

Canine Good Citizen Test

AKC CANINE GOOD CITIZEN PROGRAM
REGISTRATION FORM

Dog Number
(order tested) _____

For Testing Agency Use only:

[ ] PASS   [ ] DID NOT PASS

Owner's Name _____

_____   _____
Street Address   City/State/Zip

Phone (optional) _____

DOG'S NAME _____ AKC Number _____
as you wish it to appear on the CGC certificate

Dog's age _____ Dog's Breed _____

How much formal training has your dog had? [ ] none [ ] 1-2 obedience classes [ ] 3-4 classes

Obedience titles? _____

PROOF OF VACCINES
[ ] RABIES [ ] OTHER [ ] Licenses when appropriate

Comments:

CANINE GOOD CITIZEN OWNER'S COMMITTMENT TO RESPONSIBLE DOG OWNERSHIP
I understand that to truly be a Canine Good Citizen, my dog needs a responsible owner. As a responsible owner, I am responsible for my dog's health, safety, and quality of life. By accepting the Canine Good Citizen certificate, I agree to be a responsible dog owner.

[ ] *I will be responsible for my dog's health needs. These include:*
- routine veterinary care including check-ups and vaccines
- adequate nutrition through proper diet, clean water at all times
- daily exercise
- regular bathing and grooming

[ ] *I will be responsible for my dog's safety.*
- I will properly control my dog by providing fencing where appropriate, not letting my dog run loose, and using a leash in public
- I will ensure that my dog has some form of identification (which may include collar tags, tattoos, or microchip ID)

[ ] *I will be responsible for my dog's quality of life.*
- So that my dog will be welcomed in our neighborhood, I will make sure that my dog never infringes on the rights of others (by barking, running loose, etc)
- I understand that basic training is beneficial to all dogs
- I will give my dog attention and playtime.
- I understand that owning a dog is a commitment in time and caring.

Owner's Signature _____ Date _____

Directions: This individual test form is kept by the test giving agency for three years from the date of the test. The information on this form is recorded on the Test Summary Form, which is sent to the AKC.

CANINE GOOD CITIZEN TEST

Pedigree
FOOD FOR DOGS

Owner/Handler's Name _____ Dog's Name _____

Registered or call name

	PASS	NEEDS TRAINING
1. ACCEPTING A FRIENDLY STRANGER This test demonstrates that the dog will allow a stranger to approach it and speak to the handler in a natural, everyday situation. Evaluator approaches and shakes hands with handler; does not touch dog.	☐	lessons 2, 5 and 6
2. SITTING POLITELY FOR PETTING This test demonstrates that the dog will allow a friendly stranger to touch it while it is out with its handler. The evaluator pets the dog and then leaves the dog and handler. The dog must show no shyness or resentment.	☐	lessons 2, 5 and 6
3. APPEARANCE AND GROOMING This test demonstrates that the dog will welcome being groomed and examined and will permit a stranger, such as a veterinarian, groomer, or friend of the owner, to do so. Evaluator inspects dog, combs or brushes lightly, examines ears and each front foot.	☐	lessons 2, 3, 4 and 6
4. OUT FOR A WALK This test demonstrates that the handler is in control of the dog. The dog may be on either side of the handler, whichever the handler prefers. There must be a right turn, left turn, and about turn, with one stop in between and one at the end.	☐	lessons 3, 7 and 8
5. WALKING THROUGH A CROWD This test demonstrates that the dog can move about politely in pedestrian traffic. Dog and handler will walk close to several people; dog may show some interest without appearing overexuberant, shy or resentful.	☐	lessons 7 and 8
6. SIT AND DOWN ON COMMAND/STAYING IN PLACE This test shows the dog has training, will respond to the handler's command to sit and down and will remain in place. Dog does sit and down, then handler walks to end of 20-ft line and returns. Handler may choose to leave the dog in sit or down for the stay.	☐	lessons 2, 4 and 5
7. COMING WHEN CALLED This test demonstrates the dog will come when called by the handler. With dog on 20-ft line from Test 6, handler walks 10-ft from the dog, turns and faces the dog, and calls the dog.	☐	lesson 1
8. REACTION TO ANOTHER DOG This test demonstrates the dog can behave politely around other dogs. Two handlers and their dogs approach, shake hands, exchange pleasantries and continue on. Dogs should show no more than a casual interest in each other.	☐	lessons 6 and 7
9. REACTION TO DISTRACTIONS This test shows the dog is confident at all times when faced with common distractions. Dog may show casual interest but may not panic, show aggressiveness, or bark.	☐	lessons 2, 5 and 10
10. SUPERVISED SEPARATION This test shows the dog can be left with a trusted person and will maintain its good manners. Dog will be on 6-ft leash; leash is held by an evaluator while handler is out of sight for 3-min.	☐	lessons 2, 5 and 11

OVERALL BEHAVIOR IN IMMEDIATE TESTING AREA. Evaluators may withhold the CGC certificate if a significant incident is observed (e.g., dog bites a person or another dog) in the immediate testing area.

To receive the CGC certificate, dogs must PASS ALL 10 ITEMS of the test.

Evaluator's signature _____ Date: _____

GK9TC2 (9/96)